FUTURE-PROOF YOUR FINANCES

FUTURE-PROOF YOUR FINANCES

THE ULTIMATE GUIDE TO RETIREMENT AND
ESTATE PLANNING FOR LONG-TERM WEALTH
AND SECURITY (2-IN-1 COLLECTION)

FINANCIAL PLANNING ESSENTIALS
BOOK 3

CALVIN BOSWELL

Book Bound
STUDIOS

May this book serve as your compass and guide to all who stand at the threshold of their financial journey. To the dreamers, the planners, and the doers—who recognize the value of a secure future and the importance of leaving a lasting legacy—this work is dedicated to you. May the pages within empower you to navigate the complexities of financial planning with confidence and foresight. Here's to building a future that is not only prosperous but also profoundly rewarding. Let this be the first step in a journey that transforms your dreams into reality.

The future belongs to those who prepare for it today.

— MALCOLM X

CONTENTS

RETIREMENT PLANNING FOR BEGINNERS

ESTATE PLANNING FOR BEGINNERS

RETIREMENT PLANNING FOR BEGINNERS

A COMPREHENSIVE GUIDE TO BUILDING
SAVINGS, MAXIMIZING INCOME, AND
ACHIEVING FINANCIAL SECURITY FOR
YOUR GOLDEN YEARS

EMBARKING ON YOUR RETIREMENT JOURNEY

Understanding the Importance of Retirement Planning

Embarking on the retirement planning journey is akin to setting sail on a vast ocean. The waters may be uncharted and the horizon distant. Still, with a sturdy vessel and a reliable compass, the journey can lead to a destination of comfort and security in your later years. Understanding the importance of retirement planning is the first step in charting your course to a fulfilling retirement.

Retirement planning is essential because it is about more than just ensuring you have enough money to live on after you stop working. It's about crafting a vision for your life that extends beyond your career. This vision encompasses financial stability and considers how you will spend your time, where you will live, and what activities will fill your days. You may be adrift without a plan, subject to economic change and personal circumstances.

The importance of retirement planning cannot be overstated. It's a process that allows you to take control of your financial future and provides peace of mind that you can maintain your standard of living when you are no longer earning a regular income. It's about ensuring that your golden years are just that—golden.

Moreover, retirement planning is not a one-size-fits-all endeavour. It requires a personalized approach that considers your unique financial situation, goals, and risk tolerance. It's about understanding how much you need to save, how to invest your savings to keep pace with or outpace inflation, and how to protect your nest egg from potential financial pitfalls.

One of the most critical aspects of retirement planning is starting early. The power of compounding interest means that the sooner you begin saving, the more time your money has to grow. Even small amounts saved regularly can accumulate into significant sums over time. Conversely, delaying your savings plan can require you to save much more aggressively later in life, which may not be as feasible or could lead to a less comfortable retirement.

In addition to saving, effective retirement planning involves managing debt, understanding your retirement income sources such as Social Security and pensions, and considering the impact of taxes on your retirement savings. It also means being prepared for unexpected expenses and understanding the healthcare costs in retirement.

As you embark on this journey, remember that retirement planning is not static. It is dynamic and should be revisited regularly to adjust for life changes, economic fluctuations, and shifts in your goals and circumstances. It's about building a flexible plan to weather the storms and take advantage of favorable winds, guiding you safely to the shores of a well-deserved and well-planned retirement.

You are better equipped to move forward with a clear understanding of why retirement planning is so crucial. The next step in your journey is to set realistic retirement goals that align with your vision and provide a tangible destination for your planning efforts.

Setting Realistic Retirement Goals

As we embark on the retirement journey, setting realistic retirement goals is the compass that will guide us through the uncharted waters of our future. It's about aligning our aspirations with our financial capabilities, ensuring the golden years are as golden as we envision them.

To begin with, let's consider what retirement means to you personally. Is it a time for relaxation and leisure, a period to explore new hobbies, or an opportunity to travel the world? It's an opportunity to volunteer and give back to the community or even to start a small business. Your retirement goals should reflect your deepest desires for this significant phase of life.

Once you've painted a picture of your ideal retirement, it's time to ground those dreams in reality. Start by assessing your current financial situation. How much have you already saved? What are your expected sources of income in retirement? These include social security benefits, pensions, investments, or part-time work.

Next, estimate the cost of your retirement dreams. If travel is a priority, research and calculate the expenses associated with your dream destinations. If you hope to relocate, consider the cost of living in the new area. Don't forget to factor in the everyday expenses—housing, food, healthcare, and insurance—that will continue into retirement.

Inflation is a silent factor that can erode your purchasing power over time. When setting your retirement goals, account for the possibility that life will cost more down the line. A general rule of thumb is to plan for an annual inflation rate of 2-3%, adjusting your savings goals accordingly.

Longevity is another critical factor. With advances in healthcare, many of us are living longer, which means we need our retirement savings to stretch further. Planning for a longer retirement ensures that you will retain your resources.

Once you've considered these factors, it's time to set specific, measurable, achievable, relevant, and time-bound (SMART) goals. For instance, instead of saying, "I want to have enough to retire comfortably," quantify what "comfortably" means to you. A SMART goal might be, "I aim to save $500,000 by the age of 65, which will allow me to withdraw $20,000 annually for 25 years in retirement."

Remember, your retirement goals aren't set in stone. Life's circumstances change, and you must review and adjust your goals periodically. A job change, an unexpected expense, or a shift in family dynamics can all impact your retirement planning. Regular check-ins on your financial progress will help you stay on track and make necessary adjustments.

In setting realistic retirement goals, you're not just dreaming about the future but actively constructing it. With each goal you set and each step you take towards it, you're building the foundation for a retirement that is as fulfilling as your working years.

The Basics of Retirement Income

Understanding the basics of retirement income is crucial. After setting your retirement goals, it's time to delve into the various sources of income that will support you during your golden years. This foundation will help you assess your financial health in the next planning stage.

Retirement income typically comes from three primary sources: **government pensions, employer-sponsored retirement plans**, and **personal savings and investments**. Each of these plays a different role in your overall retirement strategy.

Firstly, government pensions, such as Social Security in the United States, provide a foundational income covering many retirees' basic living expenses. The amount you receive is based on your earnings history and the age at which you choose to start receiving benefits. Understanding how these benefits work and what you can expect to receive is essential, as they will likely form the bedrock of your retirement income.

Secondly, employer-sponsored retirement plans, like 401(k)s or pension plans, are also significant. Suppose you have a 401(k). In that case, you've been contributing a portion of your income to this tax-advantaged account, often matched by employer contributions. On the other hand, pensions provide a fixed retirement income determined by your salary and years of service. Understanding the details of your employer-sponsored plan, including when you can access the funds and how they will be taxed, is essential for planning.

Lastly, personal savings and investments fill the gaps and provide additional income. This category includes savings accounts, individual retirement accounts (IRAs), stocks, bonds, and other investment vehicles. The income from these sources depends on the amount you've saved and how you've invested it. Managing your savings effectively involves understanding investment principles, risk tolerance, and the importance of diversification.

Remember, each of these income streams comes with its own set of rules, tax implications, and benefits. Understanding how they all fit together is essential to creating a stable and reliable income throughout your retirement.

Remember that your retirement income plan should be dynamic as you consider these income sources. It will likely change over time as your needs evolve and as you transition through different phases of retirement. Regular reviews and adjustments to your plan will help ensure that your retirement income remains aligned with your living expenses and lifestyle choices.

With a clear understanding of the basics of retirement income, you're better equipped to assess your current financial health, which is the next critical step in your retirement planning process. By evaluating your financial situation, you'll be able to identify any gaps between your expected income and your desired retirement lifestyle and make informed decisions to bridge those gaps.

Assessing Your Current Financial Health

As you stand at the threshold of your retirement journey, you must take a comprehensive look at your financial health. This assessment is not just about how much you have in your savings account; it's a holistic review of your financial landscape. Think of it as a personal balance sheet that will help you understand where you stand and what you need to do to reach your retirement goals.

To begin, let's focus on your assets. These are what you own that can be converted into cash. This includes checking and savings accounts, retirement accounts like 401(k)s and IRAs, and other investments such as stocks, bonds, mutual funds, and real estate. It's essential to get a clear picture of these resources because they will form the backbone of your retirement funding.

Next, consider your liabilities, which are your debts and obligations. This includes your mortgage, car loans, credit card debt, and other loans. Knowing what you owe is just as important as knowing what you own because these will affect your retirement savings and spending.

Once you clearly understand your assets and liabilities, it's time to calculate your net worth. Subtract your total liabilities from your total assets. This figure is a snapshot of your financial health and a starting point for retirement planning.

Now, let's delve into your income and expenses. Begin by listing all sources of income, including your salary if you're still working, rental income, dividends, and any other regular cash inflows. Then, track your expenses. It's crucial to be thorough here; account for everything from your daily coffee to your monthly mortgage payment. Understanding your cash flow is vital because it influences how much you can allocate towards retirement savings.

It's also important to consider the impact of inflation on your retirement savings. The cost of living will likely increase, and your retirement income needs to keep pace. Factor in a reasonable estimate for inflation as you plan for future expenses.

Lastly, review your insurance coverage, including health, life, and long-term care insurance. These policies protect your finances from unexpected events that could otherwise derail your retirement plans.

You're laying the groundwork for a successful retirement by assessing your current financial health. It's a process that requires honesty, thoroughness, and, sometimes, tough decisions. But remember, this is just the beginning. With a clear understanding of where you stand today, you'll be better equipped to map out the journey ahead and make the necessary adjustments to ensure your retirement is as comfortable and secure as possible.

Creating a Retirement Timeline

Having taken a clear look at your financial health, you're now ready to chart the course ahead. Creating a retirement timeline is much like mapping a long-awaited road trip; it requires understanding the starting point, destination, and milestones along the way. This section will guide you through the process of establishing a realistic and flexible timeline for your retirement.

Begin by envisioning your ideal retirement age. This is not just a number but a reflection of your career aspirations, health considerations, and personal goals. Do you see yourself retiring early to pursue hobbies or spend time with family? Or do you wish to extend your career as long as possible for personal fulfillment or financial reasons? Your target retirement age sets the stage for your planning.

Next, estimate your retirement lifespan. With advancements in healthcare, many retirees can expect to live 20 to 30 years or more post-retirement. Planning for longevity is crucial to avoid outliving your resources. Consider your family health history and lifestyle as you make this estimate, and err on the side of caution.

Break down your retirement into phases, as financial needs can change significantly over time. The early years may involve active spending on travel and hobbies, while later years might see increased healthcare costs. Understanding these phases helps in anticipating changes in cash flow needs.

With these considerations in mind, you can begin to outline your retirement timeline. Start from your current age and plot the significant financial events leading up to and through retirement. These events include paying off your mortgage, your children's graduation from college, significant birthdays, and your last day of work.

As you create this timeline, consider the financial milestones you'll need to hit to retire comfortably. These include the savings you'll need by certain ages, when to start shifting your investment strategy from growth to income, and when to begin taking Social Security benefits. Remember, these milestones should be treated as guideposts, not immovable markers. Life is unpredictable, and your timeline should allow for adjustments as circumstances change.

Finally, review your timeline regularly. Your retirement goals and financial situation will evolve as you progress through your career and personal life. An annual timeline review will help you stay on track and make necessary adjustments to account for changes in the economy, income, and personal life.

By creating a retirement timeline, you're not just planning for an event in the distant future; you're taking active steps to ensure your golden years are as secure and enjoyable as possible. With a clear path, you can proceed confidently, knowing that each step you take brings you closer to the retirement you envision.

1

BUILDING YOUR RETIREMENT SAVINGS

Introduction to Retirement Accounts

As you embark on the journey of retirement planning, one of the first and most crucial steps is understanding the various retirement accounts available to you. These accounts are not just places to stash your money until you're ready to leave the workforce; they are dynamic tools designed to grow your savings through tax advantages and investment opportunities.

A retirement account is a financial plan that allows you to set aside funds for your golden years. The beauty of these accounts lies in their preferential tax treatment, which helps your savings to grow more efficiently than they might in a standard savings account. There are several types of retirement accounts, and while they all serve the same general purpose, they differ in contribution limits, tax implications, and withdrawal rules.

The most common types of retirement accounts include Individual Retirement Accounts (IRAs), 401(k)s, and Roth IRAs. Traditional IRAs and 401(k)s offer tax-deferred growth whereas Roth IRAs are funded with after-tax dollars—however, more on these later. Employer-sponsored plans like 401(k)s are also pivotal in retirement planning—but, again, more on these later.

As you consider which retirement accounts to use, consider your current financial situation, tax bracket, retirement goals, and how you want to manage your taxes now versus in retirement. The choices you make can have a significant impact on the amount of money you will have available when you decide to retire.

Remember, the earlier you start contributing to these accounts, the more time your money has to grow. Even small, regular contributions can add up over time, thanks to the power of compound interest, which we will explore in the next section. By understanding the types of retirement accounts and starting to contribute to them, you're taking a vital step toward building a secure and comfortable retirement.

The Power of Compound Interest

Imagine a snowball rolling down a snowy hillside. As it rolls, it picks up more snow, growing larger and gaining momentum with every turn. This snowball effect is a perfect metaphor for compound interest, one of the most powerful forces in building retirement savings.

Compound interest occurs when the interest earned on your savings is reinvested to earn additional interest. It's interest on interest; over time, it can turn modest savings into a substantial nest egg. To harness the power of compound interest, you need to understand two key factors: the rate of return and time.

The rate of return is the percentage by which your investment grows each year. Even a tiny difference in this rate can significantly impact your savings. For example, a $10,000 investment with a 5% annual return will grow to about $26,500 in 20 years. Increase that return to 7%; the same investment swells to nearly $39,000. That's the power of a higher rate of return.

Time is the secret ingredient that makes compound interest genuinely magical. The longer your money is invested, the more time compound interest has to work wonders. This is why starting early can make such a profound difference. If you begin saving at age 25 rather than 35, those extra ten years could mean the difference between a comfortable retirement and a financially stressful one.

Let's illustrate this with an example. Two friends, Alex and Jordan, decided to save for retirement. Alex starts at age 25, contributing $3,000 annually to a retirement account with a 7% average annual return. By age 65, Alex will have contributed $120,000, but the investment will have grown to over $600,000 thanks to compound interest.

On the other hand, Jordan waits until age 35 to start saving the same amount each year under the same conditions. By age 65, Jordan will have contributed $90,000, but the account will have grown to only about $300,000. The ten-year delay cost Jordan a significant amount in potential earnings.

To make the most of compound interest, consider these practical steps:

1. **Start Early:** The sooner you begin saving, the more time compound interest has to grow your retirement savings.
2. **Save Regularly:** Consistent contributions, even negligible, can lead to significant growth over time.
3. **Reinvest Returns:** Ensure that the interest and dividends from your investments are reinvested to benefit from compounding.
4. **Be Patient:** Compound interest is a long-term strategy. Resist the temptation to dip into your savings, as this disrupts the compounding process.

Understanding and leveraging the power of compound interest is a cornerstone of retirement planning. It's a simple concept with profound implications: save early and often, and let time and the relentless force of compounding do the heavy lifting for your retirement savings.

As you consider the impact of compound interest on your retirement planning, you must make informed decisions about the types of retirement accounts you choose. Whether Roth or traditional, each account type has tax implications and growth potential, affecting how your investments compound over time. But that's another topic where we'll delve into the nuances of choosing the proper retirement account for your financial situation.

Choosing Between Roth and Traditional Accounts

As you build your retirement savings, one of the critical decisions you'll face is choosing between Roth and traditional retirement accounts. Both options offer unique benefits and can be powerful tools in your retirement planning arsenal. Understanding their differences is crucial to making an informed decision that aligns with your financial goals and circumstances.

Let's start with traditional retirement accounts, such as a traditional IRA or a 401(k). The primary advantage of these accounts is that contributions are made with pre-tax dollars, which means you can deduct them from your taxable income in the year you make them. This upfront tax break can be particularly beneficial if you're in a higher tax bracket and expect a lower one during retirement. The money in a traditional account grows tax-deferred, meaning you will only pay taxes on the gains once you withdraw the funds in retirement. However, those withdrawals are taxed as ordinary income once you start taking distributions.

Conversely, Roth accounts offer a different tax advantage, like a Roth IRA or a Roth 401(k). Contributions to Roth accounts are made with after-tax dollars, so there's no immediate tax deduction. The trade-off, however, is that the withdrawals you make in retirement are completely tax-free, provided certain conditions are met. This includes the growth of your investments, which can be a significant benefit if you expect to be in the same or a higher tax bracket when you retire. Additionally, Roth accounts do not require you to take mandatory distributions after reaching a certain age, which is a requirement for traditional accounts.

When deciding between a Roth and a traditional account, consider your current income, expected future income, tax rates, and how long you have until retirement. If you anticipate that your retirement tax rate will be lower than it is now, a traditional account might make more sense. Conversely, a Roth account could be the better choice if you expect your tax rate to be higher in retirement or prefer the certainty of tax-free withdrawals.

It's also worth noting that you don't necessarily have to choose one. Many opt to have both accounts to diversify their tax exposure. This strategy can provide flexibility when it comes to planning and taking distributions in retirement.

Remember, the decision between Roth and traditional

accounts is not set in stone. As your financial situation changes, it is beneficial to reevaluate your choice. The key is to start saving early, understand the tax implications, and adjust your strategy to maximize your retirement savings potential.

As you continue to explore your retirement planning options, it's essential to consider the role that employer-sponsored retirement plans can play in your overall strategy. These plans often come with additional benefits, such as employer matching contributions, which can significantly enhance your retirement savings efforts.

Employer-Sponsored Retirement Plans

When building your retirement savings, one of the most valuable resources at your disposal may be your employer-sponsored retirement plan. These plans, often referred to as 401(k)s, 403(b)s, or similar titles depending on your workplace, are not just a perk of your job—they are a cornerstone of modern retirement planning.

Employer-sponsored retirement plans offer a unique combination of benefits that can significantly enhance your ability to save for retirement. One of the most compelling features is the potential for employer-matching contributions. Many employers will match a portion of the money you contribute to your plan up to a certain percentage of your salary. This is free money, boosting your savings rate and helping your retirement fund grow more rapidly.

Another advantage of these plans is the high contribution limit. For 2023, the IRS allows you to contribute up to $20,500 to your 401(k) or similar plan, with an additional catch-up contribution of $6,500 if you are 50 or older. This limit is significantly higher than that of Individual Retirement Accounts (IRAs), which we will discuss later, allowing you to save more on a tax-advantaged basis.

The tax treatment of employer-sponsored plans is also a significant draw. Depending on whether you choose a traditional or Roth option within your plan—assuming your employer offers both—your contributions can either reduce your taxable income now or provide tax-free income in retirement. Traditional contributions are made pre-tax, lowering taxable income and providing tax-deferred growth. In contrast, Roth contributions are made with after-tax dollars, offering tax-free withdrawals in retirement.

It's important to note that the funds in these plans are typically invested in a selection of mutual funds, stocks, bonds, or other investment vehicles. Your plan may offer a range of investment options, each with different levels of risk and potential return. As a beginner, it's crucial to understand your own risk tolerance and investment horizon, as these will guide your selection of investments within the plan.

Enrolling in your employer's retirement plan is usually straightforward. Most employers provide an enrollment period when you first join the company; some may automatically enroll you in the plan. If you need help getting started, your human resources department can guide you on the enrollment process and the options available to you.

Once you're enrolled, managing your contributions is critical. If possible, aim to contribute at least enough to get the full employer match; not doing so would mean leaving valuable retirement dollars on the table. Over time, as your financial situation allows, consider increasing your contributions to maximize your savings potential.

In summary, employer-sponsored retirement plans are a powerful tool in your retirement savings arsenal. They offer generous contribution limits, potential employer matching, and favorable tax treatment. By taking full advantage of these plans, you can build a solid foundation for your retirement savings, setting the stage for a more secure financial future.

While employer-sponsored plans are a significant part of retirement savings, they are not the only option. It's also essential to understand the role of Individual Retirement Accounts, or IRAs, which offer additional opportunities to save for retirement with tax advantages. We'll explore the basics and benefits of IRAs in our continued discussion on building a robust retirement savings strategy.

Chapter Summary

- Retirement accounts are designed to grow savings through tax advantages and investment opportunities, with different types offering varying contribution limits and tax implications.
- Common retirement accounts include Traditional IRAs, 401(k)s, and Roth IRAs, each with unique tax benefits and rules for contributions and withdrawals.
- Early contributions to retirement accounts are crucial due to the power of compound interest, which allows savings to grow exponentially over time.
- The rate of return and the length of time money is invested are critical factors in maximizing the benefits of compound interest.
- Choosing between Roth and traditional retirement accounts depends on one's current and expected future tax rates, with Roth accounts offering tax-free withdrawals in retirement.
- Employer-sponsored retirement plans, such as 401(k)s, often include employer matching contributions and have higher contribution limits than IRAs, providing significant retirement savings opportunities.
- Contributions to employer-sponsored plans can be made pre-tax for traditional options or after-tax for

Roth options, affecting taxable income and retirement withdrawals.

- Individual Retirement Accounts (IRAs) offer additional opportunities to save for retirement with tax advantages, complementing employer-sponsored plans in a retirement savings strategy.

2

INVESTING WISELY FOR RETIREMENT

Understanding Investment Risk

When retirement planning, it's crucial to understand that investing isn't just about picking stocks or throwing money into a retirement account and hoping for the best. It's about understanding the seas you're navigating, the risks involved, and how to steer your ship wisely through them.

Investment risk is the potential for loss or the variability in the returns of your investments. It's an inherent part of investing; with it, there is potential for higher returns that can help you achieve your retirement goals. However, not all risks are created equal and don't need to be feared; they need to be understood and managed.

There are several types of investment risks that you should be aware of:

- **Market Risk:** This is the risk that the value of your investments will decrease due to economic developments or other events that affect the entire market. The 2008 financial crisis is a prime example of market risk.
- **Interest Rate Risk:** This risk is associated with fixed-income securities, like bonds. When interest rates rise, the value of existing bonds typically falls since new bonds are likely to be issued at a higher rate.
- **Credit Risk:** This is the risk that the bond issuer could default on their payments. Bonds with lower credit ratings are considered riskier but may offer higher returns to compensate.
- **Inflation Risk:** The danger here is that the purchasing power of your money declines. If your investments keep up with inflation, you could gain ground financially even if you realize it.
- **Liquidity Risk:** This is the risk that you may not be able to sell your investment at a fair price and get your money out when you want to. Some investments, like real estate, have higher liquidity risk than others.
- **Horizon Risk:** The risk that your investment horizon may be shortened because of an unforeseen event, such as job loss or illness, forcing you to sell

investments that you were expecting to hold for the
long term.

- **Longevity Risk:** The flip side of horizon risk is the
chance you will outlive your savings. This is
particularly relevant for retirees who need to ensure
their retirement savings last.

Understanding these risks is the first step in managing them.
It's not about avoiding risk altogether—that's nearly impossible
and can lead to missed opportunities. Instead, it's about finding
the right balance between risk and return that aligns with your
retirement goals, time horizon, and comfort level.

Remember, all investments carry some risk, and it's essential
to recognize that risk is a natural part of the investing process. By
acknowledging and understanding the risks associated with
investing, you can make more informed decisions that align with
your long-term retirement strategy. This knowledge will serve as
a foundation as you learn about diversification and asset
allocation, which are key strategies in managing investment risk
and are discussed in the following section.

Diversification and Asset Allocation

Now that we've grasped the concept of investment risk in the
previous section, it's time to build on that foundation by
exploring two critical strategies for managing risk and aiming for
a successful retirement: **diversification** and **asset allocation.**

Diversification is often summed up by the old saying, "Don't
put all your eggs in one basket." In the context of investing for
retirement, this means spreading your investments across various
asset classes, such as stocks, bonds, and cash, and within asset
classes, like different sectors and geographies. By doing so, you're
not overly reliant on the performance of a single investment. If
one investment or sector underperforms, another might do well,

potentially offsetting losses and reducing the volatility of your portfolio.

Think of diversification as a balancing act. If you were to walk across a tightrope with a pole, the length and weight of the pole help you maintain balance. Each investment in your portfolio acts like a weight on that pole, contributing to a steadier journey across the financial tightrope to retirement.

On the other hand, asset allocation is the process of deciding how to distribute your investments among different asset classes. Unlike diversification, which is about spreading investments within an asset class, asset allocation is about the strategic mix of different asset classes. Your asset allocation should reflect your risk tolerance, investment horizon, and financial goals.

For instance, if you're young and decades away from retirement, you might opt for a more aggressive allocation, with a higher percentage in stocks, which have historically offered higher returns but come with more volatility. As you approach retirement, you might shift towards a more conservative allocation, with more bonds and cash, which tend to offer lower returns but are generally less volatile.

It's important to note that there's no one-size-fits-all asset allocation. It's a personal decision that should be revisited periodically, especially as you reach different stages in your life or if your goals change. Moreover, asset allocation is not a set-it-and-forget-it strategy. It requires regular rebalancing to ensure your portfolio stays aligned with your desired risk level. As market movements may cause your initial allocation to drift, rebalancing helps you sell high and buy low, realigning your portfolio back to your target allocation.

Incorporating diversification and asset allocation into your retirement planning can help you navigate the market's uncertainties while keeping you on track to your long-term objectives. By understanding and applying these concepts, you can create a robust framework for your investment decisions, which we will continue to build upon as we explore the various investment vehicles available.

Remember, the key to investing wisely for retirement is not just about selecting suitable investments but also about how you structure and manage your portfolio over time.

Exploring Investment Vehicles

As we delve into the world of investing for retirement, it's essential to understand the various investment vehicles available to you. These are the tools you will use to build your retirement portfolio, and each comes with its own set of features, risks, and potential rewards. Let's explore some of the most common investment vehicles to help you grow your nest egg.

Firstly, there are stocks, which represent ownership in a company. When you buy a stock, you buy a small piece of that company. Stocks have the potential for high returns, but they also come with a higher risk level than other investment vehicles. The value of stocks can fluctuate significantly based on the company's performance and market conditions. For retirement planning, it's often wise to consider stocks as a long-term investment, allowing you to ride out the ups and downs of the market.

Mutual funds are another popular choice for retirement savings. These funds pool money from many investors to purchase a diversified portfolio of stocks, bonds, or other securities. This diversification can help reduce risk, as your investment isn't tied to the performance of a single security. Mutual funds are managed by professional fund managers, which can be a boon for investors who prefer a hands-off approach. However, it's essential to be aware of the fees associated with mutual funds, as they can eat into your returns over time.

Exchange-traded funds (ETFs) are similar to mutual funds because they offer a diversified portfolio. Still, they trade on an exchange like a stock. This means they can be bought and sold throughout the trading day at market price. ETFs often have lower expense ratios than mutual funds, making them a cost-effective option for many investors. They also offer transparency, as the holdings of an ETF are typically disclosed daily.

Certificates of Deposit (CDs) might appeal to those seeking a more conservative investment vehicle. CDs are time deposits banks offer with a fixed interest rate and maturity date. They are insured by the Federal Deposit Insurance Corporation (FDIC) up to certain limits, making them a low-risk investment. However, the trade-off for this security is typically a lower return compared to stocks or mutual funds.

Another conservative option is Treasury securities, debt instruments issued by the U.S. government. These include Treasury bonds, notes, and bills, and they are considered one of the safest investments since the full faith and credit of the U.S. government backs them. The returns on these securities are usually lower than more aggressive investments, but they can provide a stable income stream and are free from state and local income taxes.

Lastly, there are Individual Retirement Accounts (IRAs) and employer-sponsored plans like 401(k)s, which are not investment vehicles per se but accounts that hold investments. These accounts offer tax advantages that can help your savings grow more efficiently. Within these accounts, you can hold various investment vehicles mentioned above, and choosing the right mix is critical to a successful retirement strategy.

Each investment vehicle has its place in a retirement portfolio, and the right choice for you will depend on your financial goals, risk tolerance, and investment timeline. As you consider your options, remember that a well-rounded portfolio often includes a mix of these vehicles, allowing you to balance potential returns with appropriate levels of risk.

In the next part of our journey, we'll focus on a specific type of investment vehicle that plays a crucial role in many retirement portfolios: bonds. Understanding how bonds work and their benefits will help refine your retirement investment strategy further.

The Role of Bonds in Your Portfolio

When planning to retire, understanding the role of various investment vehicles is crucial. After exploring the broad spectrum of options available, it's time to focus on a critical component that often forms the bedrock of a retirement portfolio: bonds.

Bonds are loans you, as an investor, provide to governments or corporations. In return for your investment, the issuer promises to pay you back the principal amount on a specified maturity date, along with periodic interest payments, known as coupons. These fixed-income securities can serve multiple purposes in your retirement portfolio.

Firstly, bonds are traditionally seen as a safer investment compared to stocks. While they typically offer lower returns, they also come with reduced volatility. This stability is particularly appealing as you approach retirement age and your risk tolerance diminishes. The predictable income stream from bonds can provide peace of mind, knowing that a portion of your retirement funds is insulated from the extreme ups and downs of the stock market.

Another advantage of including bonds in your portfolio is diversification. By spreading your investments across different asset classes, you can mitigate risk. When the stock market is down, bonds often perform differently. This non-correlated behavior can help cushion your portfolio against significant losses.

Bonds also offer tax advantages, mainly if you invest in municipal bonds. These bonds are typically exempt from federal taxes and, in some cases, state and local taxes. This tax efficiency can be beneficial for retirees who are looking to maximize their after-tax income.

However, it's important to note that bonds are not entirely risk-free. They are subject to interest rate, credit, and inflation risks. When interest rates rise, the value of existing bonds typically falls, since new bonds are likely to be issued at higher rates. Credit risk involves the possibility that the bond issuer may default on their payments. Lastly, inflation risk is the threat that the return on bonds may not keep up with the rising cost of living.

To manage these risks, consider the duration and quality of the bonds you select. Shorter-duration bonds are less sensitive to interest rate changes, and high-quality bonds, such as those with higher credit ratings, are less likely to default.

Incorporating bonds into your retirement portfolio requires a strategic approach. You must assess your financial situation, risk tolerance, and retirement goals. A well-constructed bond portfolio can help you balance risk and return, ensuring a more stable and predictable path toward a comfortable retirement.

As you continue your retirement planning journey, remember that the investment landscape is not static. Your portfolio needs periodic adjustments to align with your evolving needs and market conditions. This brings us to the importance of rebalancing your investments, a topic we will explore in the following discussion.

When to Rebalance Your Investments

In retirement planning, understanding the role of bonds is just one piece of the puzzle. Another critical aspect is knowing when and how to rebalance your investments to maintain a healthy, risk-adjusted portfolio. Rebalancing is the process of realigning the weightings of a portfolio of assets to stay in line with your intended asset allocation.

Imagine your retirement portfolio as a garden. When you first plant it, you carefully decide how much of each type of plant (or investment) you want. Over time, some plants may grow faster than others. If left unchecked, these might overshadow the smaller plants, disrupting the balance of your garden. Similarly, one type of investment outperforms others in a portfolio. In that case, it can become a more significant proportion of your portfolio than you originally intended, potentially exposing you to more risk than you're comfortable with.

So, when should you roll up your sleeves and rebalance your investment garden? There are two main strategies to consider:

1. **Time-based rebalancing:** This approach involves checking your portfolio at regular intervals, such as annually or semi-annually, and adjusting as necessary to return to your original asset allocation. This method is straightforward and can be quickly scheduled. However, it doesn't account for significant market movements that may occur between your set rebalancing dates.

2. **Threshold-based rebalancing:** With this strategy, you decide on a specific percentage point that your assets can deviate from their target allocation before rebalancing. For example, if your target allocation is 60% stocks and 40% bonds, you might rebalance if either asset class shifts by more than 5%. This method responds more to market conditions but requires more frequent portfolio monitoring.

Regardless of your chosen strategy, it's important to remember that rebalancing can incur transaction fees and tax implications. To minimize these costs, consider using dividends or new contributions to adjust your portfolio's balance rather than selling off assets.

Rebalancing is not just about reducing risk; it's also about taking advantage of opportunities to buy low and sell high. By selling assets that have appreciated and buying those that have not, you often buy the underperforming assets at a lower price and sell the overperforming ones at a higher price.

In conclusion, regular rebalancing is a disciplined way to maintain your desired risk level and ensure that your retirement portfolio stays aligned with your long-term financial goals. It's a simple yet powerful tool in your retirement planning toolkit that can help you stay on course through the ups and downs of the market. Remember, the key to successful rebalancing is to have a clear, predefined strategy and to stick to it, allowing you to make decisions based on logic, rather than emotion.

Chapter Summary

- Investing for retirement involves understanding and managing investment risks, not avoiding them.
- Investment risks include market, interest rate, credit, inflation, liquidity, horizon, and longevity risks.
- Diversification and asset allocation are critical strategies for managing investment and balancing risk and return.
- Diversification spreads investments across various asset classes and sectors to reduce reliance on any single investment.
- Asset allocation is a portfolio's strategic mix of asset classes, reflecting risk tolerance and investment goals.
- Retirement investment vehicles include stocks, mutual funds, ETFs, CDs, Treasury securities, IRAs, and 401(k)s.

- Bonds provide a stable income stream and can be safer than stocks, offering diversification and tax advantages.
- Rebalancing investments is crucial to maintain the desired asset allocation, manage risk, and align with financial goals.

3

SOCIAL SECURITY AND OTHER RETIREMENT INCOME

How Social Security Works

Understanding the mechanics of Social Security is a cornerstone of retirement planning. As you approach this significant phase of life, it's crucial to grasp how this program operates, as it will likely form a substantial part of your retirement income.

Social Security is a federal program designed to provide

financial support to retirees, as well as to individuals with disabilities and survivors of deceased workers. The funding for Social Security comes from payroll taxes paid by workers and their employers, known as the Federal Insurance Contributions Act (FICA) tax. Suppose you've ever glanced at your paycheck and noticed a deduction for FICA. In that case, that's your contribution to the Social Security pool.

Eligibility for retirement benefits under Social Security is based on accumulating credits during your working years. As of the latest guidelines, you earn one credit for a specific amount of earnings, with the amount required for a credit subject to change each year. You can earn up to four credits per year and generally need 40 credits, equivalent to 10 years of work, to qualify for retirement benefits.

Your Social Security benefit amount is calculated based on your 35 highest-earning years. If you have not worked for 35 years, zeros are added to the equation, which can significantly lower your average. The Social Security Administration (SSA) uses a formula to determine your primary insurance amount (PIA), the basis for your benefits.

One of the most critical decisions you'll make regarding Social Security is when to start taking benefits. You can begin receiving benefits as early as age 62, but doing so will reduce your monthly benefit amount because you're taking it over a more extended period. Full retirement age (FRA) varies depending on your birth year, and it's the age at which you're entitled to 100% of your calculated benefit. For those born in 1960 or later, the FRA is 67. Suppose you need to take benefits past your FRA. In that case, your benefit will increase by a certain percentage until you reach age 70, after which there's no additional increase for delay.

It's also important to note that your Social Security benefits may be subject to federal income taxes, depending on your combined income, which includes your adjusted gross income, nontaxable interest, and half of your Social Security benefits.

Understanding these tax implications is essential for planning your retirement income strategy.

In addition to retirement benefits, Social Security also offers spousal benefits, which allow a lower-earning spouse to receive up to 50% of the higher earner's benefit at FRA, and survivor benefits, which provide support to the family members of a deceased worker. Disability benefits are also available, offering income to those who cannot work due to a qualifying disability.

As you can see, Social Security is a multifaceted program with various rules and options that can significantly impact your retirement planning. By comprehending how Social Security works, you can make informed decisions that align with your financial goals and retirement vision. With this foundational knowledge, you'll be better prepared to delve into strategies to maximize your Social Security benefits, ensuring you optimize this vital resource for retirement.

Maximizing Your Social Security Benefits

Having gained an understanding of how Social Security works, it's time to delve into strategies to maximize these benefits, which can significantly impact your financial comfort in retirement. Social Security benefits are not one-size-fits-all; they vary depending on when you start receiving them and your work history. Here, we'll explore practical steps to ensure you get the most out of Social Security.

Firstly, consider the timing of your claim. You can start receiving Social Security benefits as early as age 62, but doing so will reduce your monthly payments because you're taking them longer. For each year you delay your claim past your full retirement age (which varies depending on your birth year), your benefits will increase until you reach age 70. This increase is known as delayed retirement credits. It can be a powerful tool for maximizing your income in later years.

Next, reviewing your earnings record with the Social Security Administration (SSA) is essential. Your benefits are calculated based on your 35 highest-earning years. If there are any errors or unreported income, correcting these can increase your monthly benefit. You can check your earnings record by creating an account on the SSA website.

There are additional considerations for those who are married, divorced, or widowed. Spouses can claim benefits based on their work record or up to 50% of their higher-earning spouse's benefit, whichever is greater. Divorced individuals may also be eligible for benefits based on an ex-spouse's record if the marriage lasted at least ten years. Widows and widowers can receive survivor benefits, a significant portion of the deceased spouse's benefit. Understanding these options can help you make informed decisions that optimize your retirement income.

Another tactic is to coordinate benefits with your spouse if you're married. Couples can maximize their total benefits by staggering their claiming ages. For example, the lower-earning spouse might start benefits earlier, while the higher-earning spouse delays claiming to accrue delayed retirement credits. This strategy increases the higher earner's benefit and sets up the surviving spouse for higher survivor benefits in the future.

Lastly, it's essential to consider how working in retirement affects your Social Security benefits. Suppose you claim benefits before reaching full retirement age and continue to work. In that case, your benefits may be temporarily reduced if your earnings exceed certain thresholds. However, once you reach full retirement age, these earnings limits no longer apply, and your benefit may be recalculated to account for the months when benefits were withheld.

In conclusion, maximizing your Social Security benefits involves careful planning and a clear understanding of the rules. By considering the timing of your claim, ensuring your earnings record is accurate, understanding spousal benefits, coordinating with your spouse, and knowing how continued work affects your benefits, you can make informed decisions that bolster your retirement income. Remember, each person's situation is unique, so consulting with a financial advisor to tailor a strategy that fits your specific needs may be beneficial.

As we move forward, we'll explore other sources of retirement income, such as pensions and annuities, to provide a comprehensive picture of how to secure your financial future during your golden years.

Pensions and Annuities Explained

Beyond the foundational layer provided by Social Security, pensions and annuities stand as two critical pillars of retirement income that can offer stability and predictability. Understanding how these financial vehicles work is essential for anyone plotting toward a secure retirement.

Pensions, often associated with government and union jobs, are defined benefit plans. This means your retirement payout is predetermined based on your salary, years of service, and the specific formula your employer uses. If you're fortunate enough to have a pension, it's like having a promise from your employer to pay you a certain amount each month once you retire. This can be a powerful asset, as it provides a steady stream of income you can count on, much like Social Security, but typically from a private source.

However, pensions are becoming less common as employers shift toward defined contribution plans, like 401(k)s, which place the onus of saving and investing on the employees. If you have a pension, it's essential to understand the terms, such as whether your spouse has an option for survivor benefits and whether the pension is inflation-protected.

On the other hand, annuities are insurance products you can purchase to provide another layer of income in retirement.

You can buy an annuity with a lump sum or through a series of payments. In return, the insurance company promises to make periodic payments to you immediately or at some point in the future. Annuities can be complex, with various types offering different features, such as fixed, variable, and indexed annuities.

Fixed annuities provide regular, guaranteed payments, making them predictably similar to pensions. Variable annuities, meanwhile, allow your payments to fluctuate based on the performance of the investment options you choose, which means they can offer growth potential but also come with more risk. Indexed annuities are a hybrid, offering a combination of guaranteed minimum payments with additional earnings that may be tied to a market index.

When considering an annuity, it's crucial to understand the fees involved, the insurance company's financial strength, and the contract's specific terms, such as surrender charges and the death benefit. Annuities can be a valuable tool for guaranteeing a portion of your retirement income. Still, they're only suitable for some and can be pretty complicated.

Both pensions and annuities offer unique benefits and considerations. As you plan for retirement, weigh these options carefully and consider how they might fit into your overall strategy for income in your golden years. Remember, the goal is to build a diversified portfolio of income sources, so you rely on only a few. With careful planning, pensions and annuities can both play a role in helping you achieve a comfortable and secure retirement.

Other Sources of Retirement Income

As we navigate the retirement planning journey, understanding the various streams of income that can support you in your golden years is crucial. Beyond pensions and annuities, which provide structured payouts, several other sources of retirement income can bolster your financial Security.

Firstly, personal savings and investments play a pivotal role. These may include savings accounts, certificates of deposit (CDs), stocks, bonds, mutual funds, and exchange-traded funds (ETFs). The key to maximizing these assets is to start saving early, invest wisely, and manage your portfolio according to your risk tolerance and time horizon. Diversification across different asset classes can help mitigate risk and provide a more stable financial foundation.

Real estate investments can also contribute to your retirement income. Whether it's rental income from a property you own or profits from selling real estate that has appreciated, this can be a significant source of funds. However, it's essential to consider the responsibilities and risks associated with being a landlord and the liquidity of real estate assets.

For those with entrepreneurial spirits, a small business or a side hustle can continue to provide income into retirement. Whether consulting in your field of expertise or turning a hobby into a profitable venture, this can be financially and personally rewarding. However, planning for the eventual transition out of the business is essential, whether selling it, passing it on to family members, or winding it down.

Another often overlooked source of income is a life insurance policy. Some policies have a cash value component that can be borrowed against or withdrawn during retirement. While this should be approached cautiously, as it can affect the death benefit and may have tax implications, it can be a helpful resource in certain situations.

Lastly, you must consider any inheritances or windfalls you may receive. While these should not be relied upon as a primary source of retirement income, they can provide a comfortable cushion or enable you to leave a legacy for your heirs.

Each income source has its considerations, such as tax

implications, growth potential, and risks. It's essential to consult with a financial advisor to understand how these pieces fit into your overall retirement plan and how they can be optimized to ensure a stable and comfortable retirement.

By thoughtfully combining these various sources of income with the foundational support of Social Security, pensions, and annuities, you can create a robust and flexible financial strategy that adapts to your changing needs throughout retirement.

Integrating Social Security with Other Retirement Funds

As you embark on retirement planning, understanding how to blend Social Security benefits with other retirement funds is a pivotal step in ensuring a stable financial future. Social Security, while a cornerstone of many retirement plans, is not designed to be the sole source of income once you retire. Instead, it's intended to work with other savings and investment strategies to provide a comprehensive income stream.

To integrate Social Security effectively with other retirement funds, it's crucial to consider when you choose to start receiving benefits. The age at which you begin to collect Social Security can significantly impact your overall retirement strategy. You can start receiving benefits as early as age 62, but doing so may reduce your monthly benefit amount. On the other hand, delaying benefits until your full retirement age—or even up to age 70— can increase your monthly payments.

When planning the integration, evaluating your entire retirement portfolio is essential. This includes personal savings, such as 401(k) plans, IRAs, pensions, and any other investments or income sources you may have. Each of these will play a role in determining the optimal time to tap into Social Security.

One strategy to consider is using your retirement savings to bridge the gap if you delay Social Security benefits. Doing so allows your Social Security benefits to grow while drawing from your other funds. However, this approach requires careful planning to ensure that your savings are sufficient to support you during this period and that your resources are manageable.

Another essential aspect to consider is tax implications. Social Security benefits may be taxable depending on your combined income, which includes adjusted gross income, nontaxable interest, and half of your Social Security benefits. Understanding how your other retirement income sources will affect your tax situation is essential, as it may influence the decision on when to begin taking Social Security benefits.

Additionally, if you plan to work during retirement, you should know how your earnings may affect your Social Security benefits. Suppose you're younger than full retirement age and earn more than the yearly earnings limit. In that case, your Social Security benefits may be reduced. However, once you reach full retirement age, you can earn any amount without affecting your Social Security benefits.

In summary, integrating Social Security with other retirement funds requires a personalized approach that considers your financial needs, life expectancy, and the impact on your overall tax situation. It's a balancing act between the present and the future, ensuring you have enough income to enjoy your retirement years while preserving your financial resources for the long term. Working with a financial advisor can help you navigate these decisions and develop a tailored plan that aligns with your retirement goals.

Chapter Summary

- Social Security is a federal program funded by payroll taxes that provides financial support to retirees, disabled individuals, and survivors of deceased workers.

- Eligibility for retirement benefits is based on credits earned during working years, with 40 credits (10 years of work) typically needed to qualify.

- Benefits are calculated from the 35 highest-earning years, and starting benefits early (age 62) reduces the monthly amount while delaying past full retirement age (FRA) increases it.

- Social Security benefits may be taxed depending on combined income, and the program also offers spousal, survivor, and disability benefits.

- Maximizing benefits involves considering the timing of claims, ensuring accurate earnings records, understanding spousal benefits, and coordinating with a spouse's benefits.

- Pensions are defined benefit plans providing a predetermined monthly payout, while annuities are insurance products offering periodic payments.

- Other retirement income sources include personal savings, investments, real estate, small businesses, life insurance policies, and inheritances.

- Integrating Social Security with other retirement funds involves careful planning around the timing of benefits, tax implications, and the use of personal savings to delay claiming Social Security potentially.

4

TAX PLANNING FOR RETIREMENT

Understanding Retirement Tax Implications

In retirement planning, it's essential to grasp the tax implications that come with it. Unfortunately, taxes don't retire when you do, and understanding how they can affect your retirement income is crucial in ensuring a comfortable retirement.

Firstly, it's essential to recognize that not all retirement income is taxed equally. The government offers certain tax breaks on retirement savings to encourage individuals to save for their golden years. However, once you start withdrawing from your retirement funds, those withdrawals are often considered taxable income.

The type of retirement account you have plays a significant role in how your savings are taxed. Traditional retirement accounts like 401(k)s and traditional IRAs offer tax benefits upfront. Contributions to these accounts are made with pre-tax dollars, which means they reduce your taxable income for the year you contribute. However, when you retire and begin to take distributions, those withdrawals are taxed as ordinary income.

On the other hand, Roth IRAs and 401(k)s are funded with after-tax dollars. This means you don't get a tax deduction for your contributions. The trade-off is that these accounts offer tax-free growth and tax-free withdrawals in retirement, provided certain conditions are met.

It's also worth noting that the timing of your withdrawals can have tax implications. For most retirement accounts, you must start taking minimum distributions, or Required Minimum Distributions (RMDs), by age 72. Not taking these distributions on time can result in hefty penalties.

Another aspect to consider is the tax bracket you expect to be in during retirement. If you anticipate a lower tax bracket, the upfront tax break from a traditional retirement account might be more beneficial. Conversely, if you expect to be in a higher tax bracket, the tax-free withdrawals from a Roth account could be more advantageous.

Social Security benefits also come with their own set of tax rules. Depending on your total income in retirement, a portion of your Social Security benefits may be taxable. Planning your retirement income strategically can help minimize the taxes on these benefits.

Lastly, it's essential to consider the impact of state taxes on your retirement income. Some states offer generous tax breaks for retirees, including no tax on Social Security benefits or exemptions on other types of retirement income. Others may have more stringent tax policies.

In summary, understanding the tax implications of your retirement savings and income is vital to retirement planning. By being aware of how different types of retirement accounts are taxed, the rules around withdrawals, and the potential taxes on Social Security benefits, you can make informed decisions that will help maximize your retirement income and minimize your tax liability. With careful planning and a solid strategy, you can navigate the tax landscape of retirement and secure a more financially stable future.

Tax-Advantaged Retirement Accounts

It's essential to understand the role of tax-advantaged retirement accounts when thinking about retirement planning. These financial vehicles are designed to encourage retirement savings by offering tax benefits that can significantly impact your long-term savings growth. Let's explore the most common types of these accounts and how they can be integrated into your retirement strategy. Note that many of these accounts have been mentioned earlier.

Firstly, we have the traditional Individual Retirement Account (IRA). Contributions to a traditional IRA may be tax-deductible depending on your income, filing status, and other factors. The money in the account grows tax-deferred, meaning you won't pay taxes on the gains until you withdraw the funds in retirement. This can be a powerful tool because it allows your investments to compound over time without the drag of annual taxes.

Another option is the Roth IRA, which takes a different approach. Contributions to a Roth IRA are made with after-tax dollars, meaning you don't get an immediate tax deduction.

However, the trade-off is that the withdrawals you make after age 59½ are tax-free, provided the account has been open for at least five years. This can be particularly advantageous if you expect to be in a higher tax bracket in retirement or prefer the certainty of tax-free income later on.

For those who are employed, 401(k) plans are a staple of retirement savings. Offered by many employers, these plans allow you to contribute pre-tax income directly from your paycheck, which then grows tax-deferred. Some employers even match a portion of your contributions, accelerating your savings. Similar to a traditional IRA, you'll pay taxes on the money when you withdraw it in retirement. There are also Roth 401(k) options that mirror the tax treatment of Roth IRAs, offering tax-free withdrawals in exchange for preceding a tax deduction on contributions.

The Simplified Employee Pension (SEP) IRA and the Savings Incentive Match Plan for Employees (SIMPLE) IRA are tailored options for small business owners and self-employed individuals. SEP IRAs allow for higher contribution limits than traditional IRAs, making them suitable for those with higher incomes looking to save more for retirement. SIMPLE IRAs are designed for small businesses and offer employer and employee contributions, providing a collaborative approach to retirement savings.

It's also worth noting that Health Savings Accounts (HSAs) can be a part of your retirement tax strategy. While HSAs are primarily intended for medical expenses, they offer triple tax advantages: contributions are tax-deductible, the money grows tax-free, and withdrawals for qualified medical expenses are tax-free. After age 65, you can withdraw funds for any purpose without penalty. However, you'll pay income taxes on withdrawals not used for qualified medical expenses.

Each account has its rules regarding contributions, income limits, and withdrawals. When choosing the proper tax-advantaged retirement account, consider your current tax bracket, expected future income, and whether you prefer to pay taxes now or later. The goal is to minimize your tax burden throughout your lifetime, not just in the current year.

By strategically using these tax-advantaged accounts, you can build a retirement savings plan that supports your future financial security and optimizes your tax situation. Remember, the key is to start early and contribute consistently, allowing the power of tax-deferred or tax-free growth to work in your favor over the long term. With careful planning and an understanding of these accounts, you can confidently navigate the path to a comfortable retirement.

Strategies for Tax-Efficient Withdrawals

Understanding how to manage your nest egg tax efficiently is crucial as we navigate the retirement planning journey. After all, it's not just what you save but what you keep after taxes that counts. Let's delve into some strategies that can help you maximize your retirement income by minimizing the tax impact.

Firstly, consider the timing of your withdrawals. Suppose you have a mix of tax-deferred (like traditional IRAs or 401(k)s) and tax-free accounts (such as Roth IRAs). In that case, you have some control over your taxable income each year. A common strategy is to pull funds from your tax-deferred accounts up to the top of a tax bracket, ensuring you're not tipping into a higher bracket with additional withdrawals. Then, you can supplement your income with tax-free withdrawals from a Roth IRA, which do not count towards your taxable income.

Another critical strategy is to manage your required minimum distributions (RMDs). Once you reach age 72, you must start taking RMDs from your tax-deferred accounts. These mandatory withdrawals can push you into a higher tax bracket. However, suppose you start taking distributions in your 60s. In that case, you can spread the taxable income over more years, potentially reducing the yearly tax hit.

Consider the potential benefits of converting a traditional IRA to a Roth IRA. This move can be advantageous if you expect to be in a higher tax bracket in the future or if you want to leave tax-free money to your heirs. The conversion will trigger a tax bill, but the money grows tax-free, and withdrawals are tax-free in retirement.

Asset location is another aspect of tax-efficient withdrawal strategies. It involves being strategic about where you hold different types of investments. For example, it's generally more tax-efficient to hold income-generating investments, like bonds, in tax-deferred accounts, where the interest they generate won't be taxed until you withdraw the money. Conversely, holding investments that generate capital gains, like stocks, in taxable accounts can be beneficial since long-term capital gains are taxed at lower rates than ordinary income.

Lastly, pay attention to the impact of state taxes on your retirement withdrawals. If you live in a state with high-income taxes, it might be worth considering how this affects your withdrawal strategy. In some cases, relocating to a state with lower or no income tax could significantly reduce your overall tax burden.

By weaving together these strategies, you can create a tapestry of tax-efficient withdrawals that support a more secure and enjoyable retirement. Remember, the goal is to manage your taxes throughout retirement, not just in the year you retire or when you turn 72. With careful planning and foresight, you can stretch your retirement dollars further and enjoy the fruits of your labor with fewer tax worries.

The Role of Health Savings Accounts (HSAs)

As you navigate the journey toward retirement, understanding the various tools at your disposal for tax planning is crucial. One such tool that often flies under the radar is one that we mentioned in the section before the last: the Health Savings Account or HSA. An HSA is a way to pay for medical expenses and a strategic component in your retirement tax planning arsenal.

An HSA is a tax-advantaged savings account to help individuals save for future medical costs. To be eligible, you must be enrolled in a high-deductible health plan (HDHP). The beauty of an HSA lies in its triple tax advantage: contributions are tax-deductible, the money grows tax-free, and withdrawals for qualified medical expenses are also tax-free.

For those looking toward retirement, an HSA can serve a dual purpose. Initially, it acts as a buffer for current medical expenses, easing the strain on your regular budget. However, its long-term value should be considered. As you age, healthcare costs can become one of the most significant expenses during retirement. An HSA allows you to build a dedicated nest egg for these costs, separate from your other retirement accounts.

The tax benefits of an HSA are particularly compelling. Contributions made to your HSA can be deducted from your taxable income, reducing your overall tax burden for the year. This deduction is available whether you itemize deductions or not. Moreover, the funds in your HSA grow tax-free, which means any interest, dividends, or capital gains accumulate without being subject to tax, much like the growth in a traditional IRA or 401(k).

When it comes to withdrawals, they are not taxed as long as they are used for qualified medical expenses. This includes many costs, from doctor's visits and prescriptions to dental and vision care. Notably, using the funds within a specific time frame is optional. This means you can contribute to your HSA during your working years and allow the account to grow until you need the funds in retirement.

One of the features of Health Savings Accounts (HSAs) is that after you reach age 65, you can withdraw funds for any purpose without incurring a 20% penalty that applies to non-qualified withdrawals before that age. However, suppose the withdrawal is not used for qualified medical expenses. In that case, it will be taxed as income, similar to withdrawals from a traditional IRA. This flexibility adds another layer to your retirement income strategy, providing an additional pool of funds that can be used for non-medical expenses, though with the caveat of being subject to income tax.

It's also worth noting that unlike a Flexible Spending Account (FSA), which has a "use it or lose it" policy, an HSA is portable and rolls over from year to year. If you change jobs or retire, the account remains with you.

Incorporating an HSA into your retirement planning requires a thoughtful approach. Consider how much to contribute each year, considering the annual limits the IRS sets. Also, consider your anticipated healthcare needs and how they may evolve as you age. Balancing contributions to your HSA with contributions to other retirement accounts is critical, as you want to ensure a well-rounded approach to your future financial security.

As you plan for a stable and secure retirement, remember that an HSA is more than just a way to cover current medical expenses—it's a powerful tool that can help you manage your long-term health costs while providing tax benefits that bolster your retirement savings strategy. With careful planning and strategic use, an HSA can be integral to ensuring a comfortable retirement.

Estate Planning and Tax Considerations

As we pivot from the topic of Health Savings Accounts, which offer their own set of tax advantages for medical expenses, let's delve into the realm of estate planning and its tax considerations. Estate planning is a crucial component of retirement planning that can significantly impact the financial legacy you leave behind. It's not just for the wealthy; everyone can benefit from a well-thought-out estate plan.

Firstly, it's essential to understand that estate planning involves more than just drafting a will. It encompasses a range of strategies to manage your assets in life and control their distribution after your passing. A comprehensive estate plan can minimize the tax burden on your heirs, fulfill your wishes, and provide for any dependents you may leave behind.

One of the key tax considerations in estate planning is the federal estate tax, which is levied on the transfer of the taxable estate of a deceased person. As of the time of writing, there is a significant exemption limit before the estate tax kicks in. Still, it's essential to stay updated on current laws as these can change with new legislation.

In addition to federal estate taxes, some states have their own estate or inheritance taxes, which may come with different exemption thresholds. It's crucial to be aware of your state's rules and plan accordingly. Strategies to mitigate these taxes include gifting assets during your lifetime, which can reduce the size of your estate subject to taxation, and setting up trusts that can offer various tax advantages.

Another aspect to consider is the use of beneficiary designations. Assets like retirement accounts and life insurance policies allow you to name beneficiaries directly. These designations typically override what's stated in a will, so keeping them updated and aligned with your estate planning goals is vital.

Furthermore, the tax basis of inherited assets is another important consideration. Generally, heirs receive a "step-up" as a basis for inherited assets, meaning they're valued as of the date of the deceased's death for tax purposes. This can significantly reduce capital gains taxes if the assets are appreciated over time and sold by the heirs.

Lastly, it's essential to consult with a financial advisor or estate planning attorney who can help you navigate the complexities of estate taxes and assist in crafting a plan that suits your needs. They can provide guidance on the use of trusts, charitable giving strategies, and other tools that can be employed to create a tax-efficient estate plan.

Remember, estate planning is not a one-time task but an ongoing process that should be revisited regularly as tax laws and personal circumstances change. By taking a proactive approach to estate planning and understanding the tax implications, you can ensure that your retirement planning is robust and comprehensive and leaves a lasting, positive impact on your loved ones.

Chapter Summary

- Retirement income is taxed differently, and understanding these implications is critical to a comfortable retirement.
- Traditional retirement accounts like 401(k)s and IRAs offer tax benefits upfront but are taxed upon withdrawal.
- Roth IRAs and 401(k)s are funded with after-tax dollars and offer tax-free growth and withdrawals under certain conditions.

- Withdrawals from retirement accounts are often required by age 72, and timing can affect tax brackets and liabilities.
- Social Security benefits may be taxable depending on total income, and state taxes can also impact retirement income.
- Tax-advantaged retirement accounts, such as traditional and Roth IRAs, 401(k)s, SEP IRAs, SIMPLE IRAs, and HSAs, offer various benefits and should be chosen based on individual circumstances.
- Strategies for tax-efficient withdrawals include managing the timing and types of accounts withdrawn from, considering Roth conversions, and understanding asset location.
- Estate planning is essential for managing assets and minimizing tax burdens for heirs, involving wills, trusts, gifting, and keeping up with tax law changes.

5

HEALTHCARE IN RETIREMENT

Estimating Healthcare Costs in Retirement

As you approach retirement, healthcare is one of the most significant expenses you'll need to plan for. Unlike your younger years, when an employer's health plan may have covered you, retirement brings a new landscape of medical costs that can impact your savings if not appropriately anticipated. To ensure a comfortable retirement, estimating your healthcare costs is a crucial step in your planning process.

Firstly, it's essential to understand that healthcare costs in retirement can vary widely depending on your health, location, and the level of care you require. However, there are some everyday expenses that most retirees can expect to face. These include Medicare Part B and Part D premiums (more on these later), out-of-pocket expenses for co-pays, deductibles, and services not covered by Medicare, as well as costs for supplemental insurance policies.

To get a realistic estimate of your healthcare costs in retirement, start by looking at the current costs of healthcare services and the rate at which they have been increasing. Historically, healthcare costs have risen faster than general inflation, so it's wise to factor in a higher rate of increase for these expenses.

Next, consider your own health status and family medical history. You may face higher healthcare costs if you have chronic conditions or a family history of certain diseases. It's also essential to consider the potential need for long-term care, which can be one of retirement's most significant healthcare-related expenses. Long-term care insurance can help mitigate these costs, but premiums for such policies should be included in your calculations.

Remember to account for the coverage gaps in Medicare. While Medicare will cover many of your healthcare needs, it doesn't cover everything. For example, dental, vision, and hearing services are typically not covered, and traditional Medicare does not cover long-term care. This is where supplemental insurance, often called Medigap, can help fill in the gaps, but at an additional cost.

When estimating your healthcare costs, use available tools and resources. Many online calculators can help you project your healthcare expenses based on your age, health status, and other factors. Additionally, speaking with a financial planner specializing in retirement healthcare can provide personalized insights and help you create a more accurate and comprehensive healthcare budget.

Finally, as you estimate your healthcare costs, reviewing these estimates regularly is essential. As you get closer to retirement and once you are retired, your health needs may change, and healthcare policies and costs may also evolve. Regularly updating your estimates will help you stay on top of your expenses and adjust your savings and investment strategies accordingly.

By carefully estimating your healthcare costs in retirement, you'll be better prepared to enjoy your golden years without the stress of unexpected medical expenses. With a clear understanding of what to expect, you can focus on maintaining your health and well-being, knowing that you've planned wisely for the financial aspect of your healthcare needs.

Medicare Basics

As you edge closer to retirement, understanding the basics of Medicare becomes increasingly essential. Medicare is the federal health insurance program for people who are 65 or older, certain younger people with disabilities, and people with End-Stage Renal Disease (permanent kidney failure requiring dialysis or a transplant). It's a critical component of your retirement healthcare planning, and getting to grips with its structure will help you estimate your healthcare costs and decide on supplemental insurance options.

Medicare is divided into four parts, each covering different services:

- **Medicare Part A (Hospital Insurance):** This part covers inpatient hospital stays, care in a skilled nursing facility, hospice care, and some home health care. Most people don't pay a premium for Part A because they or their spouse have already paid into the system through payroll taxes during their working years.

- **Medicare Part B (Medical Insurance):** Part B covers doctors' services, outpatient care, medical supplies, and preventive services. Unlike Part A, Part B requires a monthly premium based on your income. The standard premium amount changes yearly, and you may pay more if your income is above a certain threshold.

- **Medicare Part C (Medicare Advantage Plans):** These are health plan options approved by Medicare but run by private companies. They are an alternative to Original Medicare (Parts A and B), often including additional benefits like vision, hearing, dental, and health and wellness programs. Most also include Medicare prescription drug coverage (Part D).

- **Medicare Part D (prescription drug coverage):** Part D adds prescription drug coverage to Original Medicare, some Medicare Cost Plans, some Medicare Private-Fee-for-Service Plans, and Medicare Medical Savings Account Plans. These plans are offered by insurance companies and other private companies approved by Medicare.

Enrollment in Medicare is not automatic for everyone. Suppose you are already receiving Social Security benefits. In that case, you will be enrolled automatically in Parts A and B starting the first day of the month you turn 65. Suppose you are not receiving Social Security benefits. In that case, you'll need to sign up for Medicare during your Initial Enrollment Period, which begins three months before you turn 65 and ends three months after that month.

It's essential to sign up for Medicare as soon as you're eligible because if you enroll late, you may have to pay a late enrollment penalty, which could increase your premiums for Part B and Part D. There are specific special enrollment periods for those who are still working and covered under an employer's group health plan, or for those who experience other life changes.

Understanding the basics of Medicare is just the start. You'll also need to consider the additional costs that aren't covered by Medicare, such as copayments, coinsurance, and deductibles. These out-of-pocket costs can add up, highlighting the importance of considering supplemental health insurance to help cover what Medicare does not. You can better plan for a secure and healthy retirement with a solid grasp of Medicare's structure and costs.

Supplemental Health Insurance Options

Understanding Medicare is crucial as you approach retirement, but it's equally important to recognize that Medicare doesn't cover everything. Many retirees turn to supplemental health insurance options to bridge the gaps in coverage and protect against unforeseen health-related expenses. These options can help manage the costs that Medicare does not fully cover, such as copayments, coinsurance, and deductibles.

Medigap, or Medicare Supplement Insurance, is a popular supplemental option. Medigap policies are sold by private insurance companies and are designed to work alongside your Original Medicare (Parts A and B). These policies help pay some healthcare costs that Original Medicare doesn't cover. Several Medigap plans are available, each labeled with a different letter that offers a different level of coverage. It's essential to compare the plans carefully and choose one that fits your health needs and budget.

Another option to consider is Medicare Advantage Plans or

Medicare Part C. Private companies approved by Medicare offer these plans and provide all your Part A and Part B coverage. Medicare Advantage Plans may offer extra coverage, like vision, hearing, dental, and health and wellness programs. Most include Medicare prescription drug coverage (Part D). These plans often have networks, so you'll need to ensure your preferred doctors and hospitals are covered under your chosen plan.

For prescription drug coverage, you might consider a Medicare Prescription Drug Plan, also known as Part D. These plans add drug coverage to Original Medicare, some Medicare Cost Plans, some Medicare Private-Fee-for-Service Plans, and Medicare Medical Savings Account Plans. If you have Original Medicare and want drug coverage, you must join a separate Medicare Prescription Drug Plan. These plans vary in cost and drugs covered.

If you or your spouse worked for the government, you might be eligible for the Federal Employees Health Benefits Program. This program offers various plans and options that can be a valuable supplement to Medicare.

When considering supplemental health insurance, evaluating your current health needs, financial situation, and risk tolerance is crucial. Costs vary widely depending on the plan, coverage, and where you live. Review each plan's details, including the premium, deductible, and out-of-pocket maximums, to understand how they fit into your retirement budget.

Remember, the best time to enroll in these supplemental plans is during your initial enrollment period for Medicare, as you may face limited choices or higher premiums if you decide to enroll later. Planning and understanding all your options will help ensure you have the coverage you need to enjoy a healthy and financially secure retirement.

As you continue to navigate the complexities of healthcare in retirement, it's also essential to consider the potential need for long-term care and how it can impact your financial planning.

Long-term care insurance is a topic that warrants careful consideration, as it can play a significant role in your overall retirement strategy.

Long-Term Care Insurance

As we navigate the golden years, one aspect of healthcare that often comes into sharper focus is the potential need for long-term care. Long-term care encompasses a range of services and supports you may require to meet your care needs over a long period. Unlike traditional health insurance, long-term care insurance is designed to cover long-term services, including personal and custodial care, in various settings, such as your home, a community organization, or other facilities.

For many retirees, the question isn't about whether they'll need long-term care but how they'll pay for it if they do. Medicare, the federal health insurance program for seniors, provides limited coverage for long-term care. Medicaid covers such services and requires you to deplete most of your resources before you qualify. This is where long-term care insurance can play a pivotal role.

Long-term care insurance policies can help manage the financial risk of extended care that can otherwise quickly deplete retirement savings. These policies typically cover the cost of care not covered by health insurance, Medicare, or Medicaid, including assistance with activities of daily living such as bathing, dressing, eating, and using the restroom.

When considering long-term care insurance, it's essential to understand the types of policies available:

- **Traditional Policies:** These are stand-alone long-term care policies that require you to pay a premium over time. If you need long-term care, the policy pays out a daily or monthly benefit. If you never need the care, there is no return on the premiums paid.

- **Hybrid Policies:** These combine long-term care and life insurance. You pay a lump sum or make periodic payments, and if you need long-term care, the policy provides a benefit. If you don't need the care, the policy pays out a death benefit to your beneficiaries.
- **Short-Term Care Policies:** These are similar to traditional long-term care policies but have a shorter benefit period, typically one year or less.

When shopping for long-term care insurance, consider the following factors:

- **Age and Health:** The best time to buy a policy is when you are relatively young and healthy. Premiums rise as you age, and if you wait until health issues emerge, you may not qualify for coverage or face prohibitively high premiums.
- **Benefit Amount:** Determine how much coverage you want. This is usually expressed as a daily or monthly benefit, and it should align with the cost of care in your area.
- **Benefit Period:** Decide how long you want the policy to pay out. This could range from a couple of years to the rest of your life.
- **Inflation Protection:** Since the cost of care will likely increase over time, consider a policy that includes inflation protection to ensure that your benefits keep pace with rising costs.
- **Waiting Period:** The elimination period is when you become eligible for benefits, and the policy starts paying out. A longer waiting period can mean lower premiums, but you'll need to cover your costs.

- **Financial Strength of the Insurer:** Choose a company
  with a solid financial rating, as this indicates their
  ability to pay claims in the future.

Remember, long-term care insurance isn't the right choice for everyone. It's a complex product and requires a good deal of foresight and financial planning. Weigh the costs against the potential benefits and consider your risk tolerance and retirement savings. Consulting with a financial advisor or an insurance specialist can provide personalized advice tailored to your circumstances.

By understanding and planning for the potential need for long-term care, you can ensure that you can maintain your independence and quality of life in retirement while protecting your savings and providing peace of mind for yourself and your loved ones.

Managing Out-of-Pocket Healthcare Expenses

As we navigate the waters of retirement, a significant concern often surfaces: the management of out-of-pocket healthcare expenses. While we've discussed the role of long-term care insurance in the previous section, it's equally important to understand the broader spectrum of healthcare costs you may encounter during retirement.

Firstly, it's crucial to grasp what out-of-pocket healthcare expenses encompass. Medicare or other health insurance plans don't cover these costs. They include deductibles, copayments, and coinsurance for covered services, plus all costs for services that aren't covered.

To effectively manage these expenses, consider the following strategies:

- **Understand Medicare Coverage:** Continue familiarizing yourself with what Medicare covers and doesn't. Parts A and B cover hospital and medical costs, respectively, but they don't cover everything. For instance, routine dental and vision care should be covered. Knowing these details can help you plan for additional coverage.
- **Medigap Policies:** These supplemental insurance policies are designed to cover the "gaps" in Medicare, such as deductibles and coinsurance. Compare Medigap plans to find one that aligns with your healthcare needs and budget.
- **Medicare Advantage Plans:** Alternatively, you might consider a Medicare Advantage Plan (Part C) as mentioned earlier, which often includes additional benefits like dental, vision, and prescription drug coverage. These plans can reduce out-of-pocket expenses but include rules, restrictions, and costs.
- **Health Savings Account (HSA):** Again, if you have a high-deductible health plan before retiring, you might have access to an HSA. Contributions to an HSA are tax-deductible and grow tax-free, and withdrawals for qualified medical expenses are tax-free. If you're eligible, maximize your contributions before retirement.
- **Budgeting for Healthcare:** Create a detailed budget that includes healthcare costs. Use your current health status and anticipated needs to estimate expenses. Remember to factor in inflation, as healthcare costs tend to rise faster than the general inflation rate.
- **Preventive Care:** Staying healthy can help reduce healthcare costs. Take advantage of preventive services offered by Medicare, such as annual wellness visits and screenings. Preventive care can help catch health

issues early when they are more manageable and less costly.

- **Lifestyle Choices:** Adopting a healthy lifestyle can significantly impact healthcare costs. Regular exercise, a balanced diet, and avoiding tobacco can reduce the risk of chronic diseases that are expensive to treat.
- **Emergency Fund:** Even with the best planning, unexpected healthcare costs can arise. An emergency fund specifically for health-related expenses can provide a financial buffer.
- **Review and Adjust:** Your health needs will change over time, and so will healthcare policies and costs. Regularly review your healthcare coverage and expenses. Be prepared to adjust your strategies as necessary.

By taking these steps, you can exert greater control over your healthcare expenses in retirement. The goal is to balance the coverage you need and what you can afford, ensuring your golden years are as stress-free and healthy as possible. Remember, managing out-of-pocket healthcare expenses is an ongoing process that requires attention and adjustment as your needs and the healthcare landscape evolve.

Chapter Summary

- Healthcare costs in retirement can vary and include Medicare premiums, out-of-pocket expenses, and supplemental insurance costs.
- Costs have historically risen faster than inflation, so a higher rate of increase should be factored into estimates.

- Personal health status and family medical history can influence costs, and the potential need for long-term care should be considered.
- Medicare has coverage gaps, such as dental, vision, and hearing services, which may require additional Medigap insurance.
- Tools and financial planners can help estimate healthcare expenses, which should be reviewed regularly as circumstances change.
- Medicare is divided into parts A, B, C, and D, covering hospital, medical, advantage plans, and prescription drugs.
- Supplemental insurance options like Medigap, Medicare Advantage Plans, and Part D can help cover costs not fully covered by Medicare.
- Long-term care insurance is essential for covering services not included in traditional health insurance or Medicare.

6

RETIREMENT LIFESTYLE PLANNING

Envisioning Your Retirement Lifestyle

As you approach retirement, it's natural to start dreaming about your life during those golden years. Envisioning your retirement lifestyle is crucial in planning for a fulfilling and satisfying retirement. It's about more than just how you will fill your days;

it's about who you will spend them with, where you will live, and what activities will bring you joy and purpose.

Begin by considering the aspects of your current lifestyle you enjoy and would like to carry forward into retirement. Do you love the hustle and bustle of city life, or do you yearn for the tranquility of the countryside? Are there hobbies or passions you've been waiting to explore when you have more time? Perhaps you've wanted to write a novel, learn a new language, or become proficient in painting or gardening. Retirement is the perfect time to dive into these interests.

Think also about your social needs. If you thrive on social interaction, you'll want to ensure that your retirement lifestyle includes plenty of opportunities for engagement with friends, family, and community. This could mean joining clubs, volunteering, or even working part-time in a field you love.

Physical activity is another vital consideration. Regular exercise can help you maintain your health and vitality. Whether golf, yoga, swimming, or walking, find activities you enjoy and can see yourself doing regularly.

Travel often features prominently in retirement dreams. Whether it's long trips to far-flung destinations or shorter excursions closer to home, consider how travel fits into your vision for retirement. Remember to be realistic about your budget and physical capabilities when planning your adventures.

Lastly, consider your day-to-day living environment. The home and community where you choose to spend your retirement years can significantly impact your overall happiness. You can downsize to a smaller, more manageable home or opt for a retirement community offering various amenities and activities. Some retirees even live abroad, seeking new cultural experiences and potentially lowering living costs.

Remember that flexibility is critical as you reflect on your retirement lifestyle. Your interests and circumstances may change, and having a plan that can adapt to you will help ensure that your retirement years are as rewarding as possible. With careful thought and planning, you can craft a retirement lifestyle that reflects your desires and needs, setting the stage for a rich, fulfilling next chapter of life.

Relocation in Retirement: Pros and Cons

As you embark on the exciting retirement journey, one of the pivotal decisions you may face is whether to stay put or relocate. This choice can significantly impact your retirement lifestyle, so carefully weigh the pros and cons.

Here are the pros of relocating during retirement:

- **Cost of Living Adjustments:** Moving to an area with a lower cost of living can stretch your retirement savings. This could mean downsizing to a smaller home or relocating to a region with lower taxes and reduced everyday expenses.
- **Climate and Environment:** Many retirees dream of moving to a place with a more agreeable climate. Whether seeking warmer weather, less humidity, or a desire to live by the ocean or mountains, the right environment can significantly enhance your quality of life.
- **Proximity to Family and Friends:** Relocating can bring you closer to loved ones, providing emotional support and opportunities to create new memories. This can be especially important as you age and prioritize relationships.
- **Access to Healthcare:** As health becomes a more pressing concern, living in an area with excellent healthcare facilities and services can be a significant advantage. Some retirees move to be near specialized

medical centers or communities with robust healthcare options.

- **Lifestyle Opportunities:** Retirement is a time to explore new hobbies or reignite past passions. Moving to a community with like-minded individuals or a place that offers the cultural, recreational, or educational opportunities you desire can be invigorating.

Here are the cons of relocating during retirement:

- **Emotional Toll:** Leaving behind a familiar environment, cherished home, and community ties can be emotionally challenging. The sense of loss and nostalgia for the familiar can affect your well-being.
- **Moving Costs and Hassles:** Moving can be daunting, with packing, selling your home, buying a new one, and the physical and financial costs associated with the move itself.
- **Adjustment Period:** Settling into a new community takes time. Building new friendships, finding your way around, and establishing new routines can be stressful and may take longer than anticipated.
- **Unexpected Expenses:** The cost of living in a new location may have hidden expenses that you didn't account for, such as higher insurance rates, homeowner association fees, or property taxes.
- **Healthcare Disruption:** If you have established relationships with healthcare providers or are in the midst of ongoing treatments, moving away can disrupt your care. Finding new doctors and transferring medical records can be a complex process.

Before leaping to relocate in retirement, it's crucial to

consider these factors in the context of your situation. Take the time to research potential destinations, visit them, and realistically assess the impact on your finances and emotional well-being. Remember, the goal is to find a place that aligns with your envisioned retirement lifestyle, allowing you to thrive in this new chapter of life.

As you contemplate the possibility of relocating, it's equally important to consider how you'll spend your leisure time and manage travel expenses, which we'll explore in the following section. Your retirement should be a period of joy and fulfillment, and careful planning can help ensure that it is.

Budgeting for Leisure and Travel

The allure of leisure and travel often becomes more pronounced as you approach retirement. After years of hard work, the freedom to explore new places and indulge in hobbies can be advantageous. However, careful budgeting is essential to enjoy these pursuits without financial stress. In this section, we'll delve into how to effectively budget for leisure and travel in retirement, ensuring that your golden years are as fulfilling as you've envisioned.

Firstly, estimating your travel and leisure expenses as part of your overall retirement budget is crucial. Start by considering the types of activities you enjoy. Are you an avid golfer, a theater enthusiast, or a connoisseur of fine dining? You may dream of annual trips abroad or purchasing an RV to explore the country. Each activity carries a different cost profile, and recognizing your preferences will help you allocate funds appropriately.

Next, research the costs associated with your interests. If travel is a priority, look into the expenses for destinations on your bucket list. Consider travel off-season to save money, and remember to factor in travel insurance costs, which becomes increasingly important as we age. For ongoing hobbies, calculate the annual expenses for club memberships, equipment, or tickets to events.

Once you have a clear picture of the costs, it's time to integrate them into your retirement budget. A common strategy is creating a separate 'leisure account' where a portion of your retirement income is automatically deposited monthly. This method makes it easier to track leisure spending and prevents dipping into funds reserved for essential expenses.

It's also wise to consider the fluctuating nature of travel and leisure expenses. Some years, you may spend more, such as when you embark on a significant trip, while other years might be more modest. To accommodate this, you might adopt a multi-year budgeting approach, allowing unused funds from one year to roll over into the next.

Take notice of the potential for unexpected opportunities or changes in interests. A flexible budget can accommodate the occasional splurge or pursuing a new hobby. Additionally, staying informed about discounts for seniors, such as reduced admission fees to parks and museums or travel deals, can stretch your leisure budget further.

Remember, the goal of budgeting for leisure and travel in retirement isn't to restrict your enjoyment but to ensure that you can savor these experiences without financial worry. By planning and setting realistic budgetary boundaries, you can look forward to a retirement filled with the activities and adventures that bring you the most joy.

Staying Active and Engaged

As you transition from the working phase of your life into retirement, it's essential to recognize that staying active and engaged is not just a matter of filling time. It's about nurturing your well-being, both physically and mentally. The newfound freedom of retirement offers a blank canvas upon which you can paint a vibrant, fulfilling, and purposeful lifestyle.

First and foremost, consider the activities that have always brought you joy or those you've yearned to explore but never had the time for. Retirement is the perfect opportunity to dive into these interests. Whether gardening, painting, learning a musical instrument, or writing your memoirs, these activities can provide a sense of accomplishment and joy.

Physical activity is another critical component of an active retirement lifestyle. Regular exercise, tailored to your abilities and interests, can help maintain your health, flexibility, and balance. Joining a local gym, taking up yoga or tai chi, or simply going for daily walks can significantly affect how you feel. Moreover, these activities often provide social benefits, allowing you to connect with others with similar interests.

Social engagement is just as critical as physical activity. Staying connected with friends, family, and your community can help ward off feelings of isolation and loneliness that some retirees experience. Volunteer work is a fantastic way to stay engaged. It helps you give back to the community and provides a sense of purpose and connection. Look for opportunities in local schools, hospitals, or non-profit organizations that resonate with your values and skills.

Learning doesn't stop when your career does. Retirement can be a time of intellectual exploration. Consider enrolling in courses at a local community college or university. Many institutions offer programs specifically for seniors or allow them to audit classes at a reduced rate. Alternatively, online platforms provide a wealth of knowledge on virtually any topic imaginable, from history to computer programming.

Lastly, take into account the importance of downtime. While staying active is crucial, so is taking the time to relax and rejuvenate. Reading, meditating, or enjoying a quiet afternoon in your favorite park are all valuable activities. Balance is vital in retirement, as in any stage of life.

By integrating a mix of physical, social, intellectual, and leisure activities into your retirement plan, you'll be well on your way to a retirement that is not just restful but also stimulating and rewarding. Remember, retirement is not an end but a new beginning, a phase of life where you can design your days with a blend of enjoyable and enriching activities.

Part-Time Work and Entrepreneurship in Retirement

As we embrace the concept of retirement, it's essential to recognize that leaving the workforce doesn't necessarily mean stepping away from all forms of work. Part-time work and entrepreneurship can be incredibly fulfilling components of your retirement lifestyle. Let's explore how these options can supplement your income and enrich your post-career years with purpose and passion.

Part-time work during retirement is an excellent way to stay connected to the professional world without the full-time commitment. It offers flexibility, allowing you to balance leisure with earning a paycheck. For many retirees, part-time jobs provide more than just financial benefits; they offer social interaction, mental stimulation, and a sense of social contribution. When considering part-time work, look for roles that align with your interests or past experiences. You could consult within your former industry or enjoy retail work in a field you're passionate about, like gardening or bookselling.

On the other hand, retirement can be the perfect time to unleash your entrepreneurial spirit. Starting a business can be an exciting venture, allowing you to turn a hobby or a lifelong dream into a source of income. Entrepreneurship in retirement comes with the freedom to set your own pace and make decisions that align with your desired lifestyle. Whether it's starting a small craft business, offering freelance services, or even launching a start-up, the key is choosing an endeavor that you're truly passionate about that won't overburden you.

Before diving into part-time work or entrepreneurship, it's essential to consider how this income will affect your retirement savings and tax situation. Consulting with a financial advisor can help you understand the implications and ensure your work supports your long-term financial security.

Moreover, it's crucial to strike a balance that keeps the leisure time you've earned. Retirement is your time to relax and enjoy life at a slower pace. Ensure that any work you take on enhances your life rather than becoming a source of stress.

Part-time work and entrepreneurship can be rewarding ways to complement your retirement. They provide opportunities to stay active, engaged, and financially secure. By carefully selecting work that aligns with your interests and lifestyle goals, you can craft a productive and pleasurable retirement. Remember, retirement is not the end of your working life; it's a new chapter where you can redefine what work means.

Chapter Summary

- Envisioning your retirement lifestyle is essential for a fulfilling retirement, considering factors like location, social needs, and hobbies.
- Physical activity and travel are essential aspects of retirement planning, with realistic considerations for budget and health.
- Relocating in retirement has pros, such as lower living costs and better climate, and cons, like emotional challenges and moving expenses.
- Budgeting for leisure and travel is crucial to enjoying these activities without financial stress, including

estimating costs and creating a separate leisure account.

- Staying active and engaged through hobbies, exercise, socializing, and learning is vital for physical and mental well-being in retirement.
- Downtime is also essential for relaxation, rejuvenation, and a balanced retirement lifestyle.
- Part-time work and entrepreneurship can provide financial benefits, purpose, and passion in retirement, with flexibility and alignment with personal interests.
- It's essential to consider the impact of additional income on retirement savings and taxes and to ensure work doesn't compromise leisure time.

7

PROTECTING YOUR RETIREMENT SAVINGS

Insurance Needs for Retirees

As you approach retirement, it's crucial to understand that your insurance needs may change significantly. While working, you might have relied on employer-provided health insurance, life insurance, and perhaps even disability coverage. However, as you transition into retirement, these safety nets often disappear, necessitating a thorough review of your insurance requirements to protect your hard-earned retirement savings.

Firstly, health insurance becomes a pivotal concern for retirees. Suppose you retire before you are eligible for Medicare at age 65. In that case, you'll need to find an alternative form of health insurance to bridge the gap. Even after you qualify for Medicare, you may want to consider purchasing supplemental insurance, often referred to as Medigap, to cover expenses that Medicare does not, such as copayments, deductibles, and certain types of care.

Long-term care insurance is another important consideration. The cost of long-term care can be staggering and is not typically covered by Medicare. Long-term care insurance can help protect your retirement savings from the potential financial burden of this type of care. However, these policies can be expensive, so weighing the costs and benefits carefully and considering factors such as your health history and family longevity is essential.

Life insurance needs may also change as you enter retirement. If your children are independent and your mortgage is paid off, you might not need as much life insurance as you did when you were younger. However, if you have dependents or significant debts, maintaining life insurance could be wise to protect your loved ones.

Additionally, an often-overlooked type of insurance is liability insurance. As you age, the risk of being sued for accidents on your property or as a result of your actions can threaten your retirement nest egg. An umbrella liability policy can offer extra protection above and beyond your standard homeowners or auto insurance policies.

Finally, it's essential to regularly review and adjust your insurance coverage throughout your retirement to ensure it continues to meet your changing needs. Your health situation can change as you age, and your insurance should adapt accordingly. Working with a financial advisor or insurance professional can help you navigate these complex decisions and find the best coverage.

By carefully considering your insurance needs and ensuring you're adequately protected, you can help safeguard your retirement savings against unforeseen expenses, allowing you to enjoy your golden years with greater peace of mind.

Dealing with Debt Before Retirement

One of the most crucial steps you can take to protect your nest egg is to tackle any outstanding debt. Entering retirement debt-free is not just a matter of financial health—it's also about peace of mind. Let's explore strategies to manage and eliminate debt before you bid farewell to your working years.

Firstly, it's essential to understand the types of debt you have. High-interest debt, such as credit card balances, should be your top priority. These debts can quickly spiral out of control and eat into the savings you've worked so hard to accumulate. Consider transferring balances to a lower-interest card or a consolidation loan, but only if it will help you pay off the debt more quickly and with less interest.

Next, look at any loans or mortgages you may have. While these often come with lower interest rates, they can still be burdensome in retirement. Accelerate your payments now while you have a steady income. Even small additional payments can significantly reduce the interest you'll pay over the life of the loan. You can shorten the time to pay it off.

Another critical step is to create a budget that prioritizes debt repayment. This may mean cutting back on discretionary spending or boosting your income while working. Every extra dollar you can put toward your debt is an investment in your future financial security.

It's also wise to avoid taking on new debt. As retirement nears, you may be tempted to finance that dream vacation or the new car you've been eyeing. However, remember that borrowing money now will only reduce the funds available in retirement if you must make a large purchase. Plan and save for it rather than rely on credit.

If you're struggling to manage your debt, don't hesitate to seek help. A financial advisor can provide personalized advice and help you develop a plan to get back on track. There are also non-profit credit counseling services that can assist with budgeting and debt management plans.

Finally, as you work toward becoming debt-free, it's essential to maintain a safety net. While paying off debt is a priority, you should also ensure an emergency fund is in place. Unforeseen expenses can sometimes arise, and having a reserve can prevent you from falling back into debt.

By addressing your debt before retirement, you're protecting your savings and setting the stage for a more relaxed and enjoyable retirement. With fewer financial obligations, you can focus on the activities and experiences that matter most. Remember, the freedom from debt is one of the most valuable assets you can have in retirement.

Avoiding Scams and Financial Fraud

Safeguarding your nest egg becomes paramount as you approach retirement. After all, you've worked hard to accumulate these savings, representing your financial security during your golden years. Protecting your retirement savings is critical to being vigilant against scams and financial fraud. Unfortunately, unscrupulous individuals often target retirees because they may have substantial savings and can be perceived as less savvy with new technology or financial schemes.

To help you navigate these treacherous waters, let's explore some practical steps you can take to avoid becoming a victim of financial fraud.

Firstly, educate yourself about the common types of scams that target retirees. These can range from investment fraud, such as Ponzi schemes and fake opportunities promising high returns with little or no risk, to personal scams like phishing attempts or the grandparent scam, where someone pretends to be a relative needing immediate financial help.

Be skeptical of unsolicited offers. If you receive an offer out of the blue, whether through email, a phone call, or even a knock on the door, treat it with caution. Scammers often use high-pressure tactics to create a sense of urgency, so take your time researching and thinking things over before making any financial decisions.

Protect your personal information zealously. Only give out sensitive information such as your Social Security number, bank account details, or credit card numbers if you initiated the contact and know the recipient's legitimacy. Shred documents containing personal information before disposing of them.

Verify credentials and seek independent advice. Before you invest with a new financial advisor or buy an insurance product, check their credentials with regulatory bodies such as the Securities and Exchange Commission (SEC) or the Financial Industry Regulatory Authority (FINRA). Additionally, it's wise to get a second opinion from a trusted financial advisor or a family member when considering significant financial moves.

Monitor your accounts regularly. Keep an eye on your bank and retirement accounts, looking for unauthorized transactions. Setting up alerts for large transactions can also help you stay informed of any significant changes in your account.

Finally, if something sounds too good to be true, it probably is. Be wary of any investment or opportunity that guarantees returns with no risk. The reality is that all investments carry some risk, and those promising otherwise are often red flags for fraud.

By staying informed and cautious, you can significantly reduce the risk of falling prey to scams and ensure that your retirement savings remain secure when needed. Protecting your financial well-being is about growing your savings and preventing losses through vigilance and intelligent decision-making.

The Importance of an Emergency Fund

As you embark on the retirement planning journey, it's crucial to understand that safeguarding your future isn't just about growing your nest egg but also about protecting it from potential setbacks. Establishing an emergency fund is one of the most effective ways to shield your retirement savings. This financial buffer can help you manage unexpected expenses without dipping into the retirement pot you've worked so hard to cultivate.

An emergency fund is a cash reserve readily accessible and earmarked for unforeseen events such as medical emergencies, home repairs, or sudden job loss. The importance of this fund cannot be overstated, as it serves as your first line of defense against the unpredictable nature of life. With it, you may be able to withdraw from your retirement accounts earlier than planned, which can have several adverse effects.

Firstly, early withdrawals can significantly diminish the compound growth of your savings. Remember, the money you pull out today could have grown substantially over time, potentially leaving you with a much smaller sum when you retire. Secondly, taking money out of certain retirement accounts before reaching the age of 59½ often triggers penalties and taxes, further eroding your savings.

So, how much should you aim to save in your emergency fund? A good rule of thumb is to have enough to cover three to six months' living expenses. This amount can provide a comfortable cushion, giving you the peace of mind to handle life's curveballs without jeopardizing your retirement goals.

Building an emergency fund may seem daunting, especially

starting from scratch. However, you can gradually build up this critical resource by setting aside a small portion of your income regularly. Consider automating your savings to make the process easier and more consistent. Additionally, keep these funds in a separate, easily accessible account to avoid the temptation of using them for non-emergencies.

In summary, while focusing on the long-term vision of a secure retirement is essential, take notice of the short-term necessity of an emergency fund. This financial safety net is vital to protecting your retirement savings, ensuring that when life throws you a financial challenge, you're well-prepared to face it head-on without derailing your plans.

Legal Documents to Protect Your Assets

As you diligently save for retirement, it's equally essential to safeguard your assets. While an emergency fund is a critical buffer for unexpected expenses, legal documents are the bedrock for protecting your assets and ensuring they are managed according to your wishes, both during your lifetime and after.

A will is one of the most fundamental documents in your asset protection arsenal. A will is a legal declaration by which you, the testator, name one or more persons to manage your estate and provide for the transfer of your property at death. Without a will, the state decides how your assets are distributed, which may not align with your wishes. By creating a will, you can dictate who inherits your assets, from your retirement accounts to your family heirlooms.

Another key document is a durable power of attorney. This allows you to appoint a trusted individual to manage your affairs if incapacitated. It's a common misconception that your spouse or adult children can automatically step in to make decisions on your behalf. In reality, with a power of attorney, they could petition the court to be named their guardian. This process can be time-consuming and stressful.

In addition to a power of attorney for financial matters, you should consider a healthcare power of attorney or proxy. This document appoints someone to make medical decisions on your behalf if you cannot do so. It's often paired with a living will, which outlines your wishes regarding life-sustaining treatment if you're terminally ill or permanently unconscious.

A trust might be a suitable option for those with more complex financial situations. Trusts come in various forms and can offer greater control over how your assets are distributed. For example, a revocable living trust allows you to retain control over the assets during your lifetime. It specifies how they should be handled after your death. Trusts can also help minimize estate taxes and offer protection from creditors and legal judgments.

Beneficiary designations are another critical component of protecting your retirement savings. These designations are typically found on life insurance policies, retirement accounts like 401(k)s and IRAs, and other financial accounts. Review and update these designations regularly, especially after significant life events like marriage, divorce, or the birth of a child, to ensure that your assets are passed on to the intended recipients.

Lastly, it's prudent to keep all these documents in a secure but accessible location and to inform your appointed representatives of their whereabouts. Regular reviews with a financial advisor or attorney can help ensure that your legal documents remain up-to-date with your current wishes and any changes in the law.

By taking these steps, you can rest assured that your retirement savings and other assets are protected. This provides you with peace of mind and simplifies the management of your estate for your loved ones, ensuring that your legacy is preserved according to your exact specifications.

Chapter Summary

- As retirees transition from work to retirement, they must reassess their insurance needs, as employer-provided coverage often ends.
- Health insurance is critical for retirees, especially those under 65 who aren't yet eligible for Medicare, and supplemental insurance may be needed even after Medicare eligibility.
- Long-term care insurance can protect retirement savings from the high long-term care costs, which Medicare does not typically cover.
- Life insurance needs may decrease if dependents no longer rely on the retiree's income. Still, it remains essential for those with dependents or debts.
- Liability insurance, such as an umbrella policy, can protect retirees from lawsuits threatening their savings.
- Regularly reviewing and adjusting insurance coverage is essential to meet changing needs throughout retirement.
- Working with a financial advisor or insurance professional can help retirees navigate complex insurance decisions and find the best coverage.
- Protecting retirement savings involves careful consideration of insurance needs to avoid unforeseen expenses and enjoy a more secure retirement.

8

NAVIGATING RETIREMENT
CHALLENGES

Coping with Unexpected Life Events

Life is full of surprises; not all come with a bow. As you journey towards retirement, it's crucial to acknowledge that unexpected life events can and often do occur, potentially derailing even the most well-thought-out plans. Coping with these events is not just about having a contingency plan but cultivating resilience and adaptability in your financial strategy.

One of the most common unforeseen events is a health crisis. An accident or illness can lead to significant medical expenses that aren't fully covered by insurance, and it may also limit your ability to work temporarily or permanently. To mitigate this risk, consider purchasing comprehensive health insurance and exploring disability insurance options. Building and maintaining an emergency fund can also provide a financial buffer to help cover out-of-pocket expenses without dipping into your retirement savings.

Another unexpected event could be the loss of a job. Whether due to downsizing, company closure, or other reasons, the loss of steady income can be a significant setback. If you're nearing retirement, this might mean finding a new job or adjusting your retirement timeline. To prepare for such a scenario, try to diversify your income streams. This could involve part-time work, freelancing, or passive income sources like rental properties or investment dividends.

Family dynamics can also change unexpectedly and impact your retirement planning. For instance, you might find yourself in a situation where you need to support an adult child financially, or you may need to contribute to the care of aging parents. These responsibilities can strain your retirement savings if not planned for. To address this, consider setting clear boundaries on financial support and exploring insurance products like long-term care insurance for elderly relatives.

Lastly, divorce or losing a spouse can profoundly affect your retirement plans. Not only do these events have emotional ramifications, but they can also have financial consequences, such as the division of assets or loss of a second income. Reviewing and updating your retirement plan to reflect your new circumstances is essential, and seeking professional financial advice if needed.

In all cases, the key to coping with unexpected life events is flexibility. Regularly review and adjust your retirement plan to accommodate changes in your life. Keep informed about your financial situation. Feel free to seek advice from financial advisors who can provide personalized guidance tailored to your circumstances.

Remember, while you can't predict every twist and turn life throws at you, you can prepare to navigate through them with confidence and poise. By doing so, you'll protect your retirement savings and give yourself peace of mind, knowing you're as ready as you can be for whatever lies ahead.

Managing Inflation Impact on Retirement Savings

Inflation is often likened to a silent thief that can slowly erode the purchasing power of your hard-earned retirement savings. As you embark on the retirement planning journey, understanding and managing the impact of inflation is crucial. It's not just about how much you save but also how much those savings will be worth when you need them.

To begin with, it's essential to recognize that inflation is a normal part of economic life. Prices for goods and services rise over time, meaning that the dollar you save today will likely buy less. This is particularly important for retirees, who may be on fixed incomes and have less opportunity to increase their earnings.

One of the most effective strategies to counteract inflation is to include investments in your portfolio that can grow at a rate that outpaces inflation. Historically, equities or stocks have provided returns that exceed inflation over the long term. However, they come with higher volatility and risk. Including a diversified mix of stocks in your retirement portfolio can help maintain the purchasing power of your savings.

Another approach is to consider Treasury Inflation-Protected

Securities (TIPS). TIPS are government bonds specifically designed to protect against inflation. The principal value of TIPS rises with inflation and falls with deflation, which can provide a measure of security in a fluctuating economy.

It's also wise to gradually increase your withdrawal rate to account for rising costs. A common rule of thumb is the 4% rule, which suggests withdrawing 4% of your retirement savings in the first year and then adjusting that amount for inflation each subsequent year. However, this rule is not one-size-fits-all, and you may need to tailor your withdrawal strategy based on your circumstances and market conditions.

In addition to investment strategies, staying flexible with your spending can be a powerful tool. This might mean adjusting your budget to prioritize essential expenses and finding ways to reduce costs or increase efficiency in your day-to-day life. For example, downsizing your home, using public transportation, or taking advantage of senior discounts can all help stretch your retirement dollars further.

Lastly, consider working with a financial advisor who can help you navigate the complexities of inflation and retirement planning. A professional can provide personalized advice and help you adjust your plan to address the changing economic landscape.

By taking proactive steps to manage the impact of inflation, you can better ensure that your retirement savings will support you throughout your golden years. Remember, the goal is not just to save but to maintain the value of those savings so you can enjoy the retirement you've worked so hard to achieve.

Adjusting Your Plan for Market Volatility

Market volatility can be a daunting aspect of retirement planning. The ups and downs of the stock market can significantly affect the value of your retirement savings, primarily if you are heavily invested in equities. However, with a few strategic adjustments to your retirement plan, you can navigate these choppy waters and maintain a course toward a secure retirement.

Firstly, it's essential to understand that market volatility is expected in investing. While it can be unsettling to see the value of your investments fluctuate, remember that retirement planning is a long-term endeavor. Over time, markets have historically trended upward despite short-term fluctuations.

One of the most effective strategies for dealing with market volatility is diversification. By spreading your investments across different asset classes, such as stocks, bonds, and real estate, you can reduce the risk that a downturn in any area will devastate your overall portfolio. Diversification can provide a buffer against the unpredictable nature of the markets.

Another key tactic is to have a well-thought-out asset allocation strategy that aligns with your risk tolerance and retirement timeline. As you approach retirement, it's generally advisable to gradually shift your asset allocation to include more conservative investments, like bonds, which are less susceptible to market swings. This can help protect the money you'll need to access in the near term.

Rebalancing your portfolio periodically is also crucial. This involves selling some investments that have increased in value and buying others that have decreased to maintain your desired asset allocation. Rebalancing helps you stick to your investment strategy. It can prevent you from being overly exposed to risk during market highs or lows.

An often-overlooked aspect of adjusting for market volatility is maintaining an emergency fund. Having a cash reserve can be particularly helpful during market stress, as it allows you to cover your living expenses without selling investments at a loss.

Lastly, it's important not to let emotions drive your investment decisions. Making impulsive choices during a market downturn can lock in losses and derail your retirement plan. Instead, focus on your long-term goals and consult a financial advisor to help guide you through turbulent times.

By implementing these strategies, you can create a retirement plan that is better equipped to handle the inevitable market volatility. This will allow you to focus on what truly matters: enjoying your retirement years with peace of mind, knowing you have a plan to adapt to changing financial landscapes.

Dealing with the Loss of a Spouse

The loss of a spouse is a profound event that can shake the very foundations of your life, not least of which is your financial stability and retirement planning. It's a time of deep emotional distress, and the added pressure of financial decisions can feel overwhelming. However, navigating this difficult period with care can help ensure that you remain on a stable financial path for the years to come.

First and foremost, permit yourself to grieve. Acknowledging your emotions and seeking support from friends, family, or a professional counselor is vital. Financial decisions can wait during the initial period of mourning.

Once you're ready to focus on practical matters, taking stock of your current financial situation is crucial. This includes understanding the full scope of your assets, liabilities, and income streams. You'll need to review all accounts, including bank accounts, retirement accounts, investment portfolios, and insurance policies. It's also essential to update any beneficiary designations that may have been in your spouse's name.

Social Security benefits will also need to be addressed. You might be eligible for survivor benefits if your spouse was receiving benefits. The rules surrounding these benefits can be complex, so consider consulting with a Social Security

Administration representative or a financial advisor who can guide you through the process.

Adjusting your budget is another critical step. Your household expenses may have changed, and you must create a new budget that reflects your current income and expenses. This may also be an excellent time to reevaluate your retirement goals and timelines. You may need to work a few more years than initially planned or decide to downsize your home to reduce living expenses.

Estate settlement is another area that will require attention. You'll need to locate your spouse's will and any other estate planning documents, such as trusts, and begin settling the estate. This can be a complex task, and it's often wise to enlist the help of an estate attorney to navigate the legalities and ensure that your spouse's wishes are honored.

Lastly, it's essential to review and update your estate plan. This includes your will, powers of attorney, and health care directives. It's a step that protects your assets and provides clarity and direction for your loved ones in the event of your own passing.

In dealing with the loss of a spouse, remember that you don't have to make all these decisions alone. Lean on trusted family members, friends, and professionals who can offer support and guidance. By taking measured steps, you can regain control of your financial life and continue confidently moving forward into retirement.

As you stabilize your financial footing after such a significant life change, it's also essential to consider the broader context of your retirement, including the dynamics within your family. Open communication about expectations, responsibilities, and support can ensure that your retirement years are as fulfilling and stress-free as possible.

Family Dynamics and Retirement

As we gracefully accept the changes that come with losing a spouse, we must also focus on the broader family dynamics that play a pivotal role in retirement. The family unit, often a source of support and comfort, can also present unique challenges during this phase of life. Understanding and navigating these relationships is crucial for a fulfilling retirement.

Firstly, the concept of dependency can shift significantly during retirement. If you have children, they may have reached adulthood and independence, which can alter your role within the family. This change can affect your sense of purpose and require adjusting how you interact with your children. It's essential to foster a balance between offering guidance and allowing them the freedom to make their own decisions. Additionally, the arrival of grandchildren can bring joy and new responsibilities, potentially impacting your retirement plans.

Secondly, your retirement can also affect your relationship with your siblings and extended family. You may find yourself able to care for aging relatives or support siblings going through their own life transitions. These responsibilities can be rewarding but can also add complexity to your retirement planning. Communicating openly with family members about your capacity to provide support while maintaining your well-being is essential.

Another aspect to consider is your potential financial support to family members. Whether helping a child with a down payment on a house, contributing to a grandchild's education, or assisting a sibling in need, these decisions can have significant implications for your retirement savings. It's essential to evaluate your financial situation and set clear boundaries to ensure that your generosity does not compromise your financial security.

Moreover, retirement can sometimes lead to increased time spent with family, which can be both a blessing and a source of stress. Differences in opinions, lifestyles, and values can emerge during extended family gatherings. It's beneficial to approach these situations with patience and understanding and to seek common ground that strengthens family bonds.

Finally, it's worth acknowledging that some retirees may face the challenge of feeling disconnected from family. Whether due to geographical distance, strained relationships, or the pursuit of different interests, finding ways to stay connected is essential. This could involve regular communication through phone calls, video chats, or planning family reunions. Engaging in shared activities or hobbies can also provide opportunities to create new memories and reinforce family ties.

In conclusion, retirement is not just a personal journey but one that intertwines with the lives of those we hold dear. You can navigate these challenges successfully by approaching family dynamics with empathy, clear communication, and a willingness to adapt. Remember, the goal is to build a retirement that is financially secure and rich in the relationships that matter most.

Chapter Summary

- Acknowledge that unexpected life events can affect retirement plans and cultivate financial resilience and adaptability.
- Prepare for health crises with comprehensive health insurance, disability insurance, and an emergency fund.
- Diversify income streams to mitigate the impact of job loss and consider part-time work or passive income sources.
- Plan for changes in family dynamics, such as supporting adult children or aging parents, and set financial boundaries.

- Update retirement plans after divorce or loss of a spouse and seek professional financial advice if necessary.
- Counteract inflation by investing in assets that outpace inflation, like equities and Treasury Inflation-Protected Securities (TIPS).
- Adjust for market volatility by diversifying investments, rebalancing portfolios, and maintaining an emergency fund.
- Navigate the loss of a spouse by allowing time to grieve, understand finances, adjust budgets, and update estate plans.

9

ESTATE PLANNING AND LEGACY

The Essentials of Estate Planning

As you embark on the retirement planning journey, it's crucial to understand that preparing for the future isn't just about ensuring you have enough money to live on. It's also about ensuring your assets and legacy are handled according to your wishes after you're gone. This is where estate planning comes into play, serving as a critical component of a comprehensive retirement plan.

Estate planning, at its core, is about control and care. It's legally structuring the future disposition of current and projected assets. It's not just for the wealthy; everyone has an estate, the total of all their assets, and everyone can benefit from a well-thought-out plan.

The first step in estate planning is taking stock of what you own. This includes tangible assets like your home, car, and personal possessions and intangible assets such as investments, insurance policies, and business interests. Once you have a clear picture of your assets, consider how you want them distributed.

One of the most straightforward tools in estate planning is the will. A will is a legal document that outlines how you want your property and assets to be distributed after your death. It can also specify guardians for any minor children. Without a will, the state decides how to distribute your assets, which may not align with your wishes.

However, a will is just one part of the estate planning process. Other components can include powers of attorney, allowing you to appoint someone to make decisions on your behalf if you cannot. There are two main types: a healthcare power of attorney, which covers medical decisions, and a financial power of attorney, which covers financial and legal decisions.

Another important aspect of estate planning is the designation of beneficiaries on accounts such as life insurance policies, retirement accounts, and bank accounts. These designations often override instructions in a will, so keeping them updated and in line with your estate planning goals is essential.

Trusts can be a valuable tool for those with more complex estates or specific wishes. Trusts come in various forms and can offer benefits such as avoiding probate, reducing estate taxes, and protecting assets from creditors.

Estate planning also involves considering the potential tax implications of inheritance. While not everyone's estate will be subject to estate taxes, it's essential to understand how these taxes work and what can be done to minimize them.

Lastly, reviewing and updating your estate plan regularly is vital, especially after significant life events like marriage, divorce, the birth of a child, or the acquisition of significant assets. An outdated estate plan can create confusion and conflict among your heirs. It may not reflect your current wishes or financial situation.

Remember, estate planning is a personal process and can be as simple or complex as your situation requires. It's about preserving your legacy and caring for your loved ones in the way you intend. With careful planning and the help of professionals like attorneys and financial advisors, you can create an estate plan that provides peace of mind for you and your family.

Wills and Trusts: Understanding the Basics

It's crucial to understand the foundational elements that ensure your legacy is preserved and your wishes are honored. Two elements are **wills** and **trusts**, each playing a distinct role in orchestrating your estate's future.

A will, often called a last will, is a legal document articulating your desires regarding the distribution of your assets and the care of any minor children upon your passing. It's the most basic estate planning tool, and it's essential for anyone looking to have a say in how their estate is handled after death. Without a will, the state's intestacy laws take over, and these may not align with your wishes.

Creating a will is a straightforward process requiring careful attention to detail. You'll need to appoint an executor, the person responsible for carrying out the instructions in your will. Choosing someone trustworthy and capable of managing the role's responsibilities is essential. You'll also need to be clear about who receives what, whether it's a family heirloom, a sum of money, or a piece of real estate. Being specific in your will can help prevent disputes among your heirs and ensure that your assets are distributed according to your wishes.

On the other hand, trusts are slightly more complex but offer additional benefits that a will alone cannot provide. A trust is a fiduciary arrangement allowing a third party, or trustee, to hold assets on behalf of a beneficiary or beneficiary. Trusts can be arranged in many ways and specify how and when the assets pass to the beneficiaries. Unlike wills, trusts typically avoid probate, the legal process through which a will is validated. This means that the distribution of assets can occur more quickly, privately, and often with fewer expenses and taxes.

There are various types of trusts designed to address different estate planning goals. For instance, a revocable living trust allows you to maintain control over the trust assets during your lifetime. It provides for transferring those assets after death, all while avoiding probate. An irrevocable trust, once established, generally cannot be altered, but it can offer significant tax benefits and asset protection.

When considering whether a will or a trust is more appropriate for your situation, evaluating the size and complexity of your estate, your privacy preferences, and your long-term objectives is essential. For many, combining a will and a trust is the most effective way to ensure comprehensive estate planning.

Remember, estate planning is not a one-size-fits-all process. It's a deeply personal journey that reflects your unique circumstances, values, and aspirations. As you contemplate the creation of a will or trust, it's wise to consult with an estate planning attorney who can guide you through the nuances of each option and help you craft a plan that aligns with your vision for the future.

With a solid understanding of wills and trusts, you're better equipped to make informed decisions about structuring your estate plan. This knowledge is a stepping stone to the next aspect of estate planning: designating beneficiaries for your assets and ensuring that your legacy is passed on according to your wishes.

Beneficiary Designations and Their Importance

As we delve into the intricacies of estate planning, it's crucial to understand the role of beneficiary designations and why they are a cornerstone of a well-structured retirement plan. While wills and trusts are essential for outlining your wishes, beneficiary designations are direct and often expedited means of transferring assets upon passing.

Beneficiary designations are unique in bypassing the probate process, the legal procedure through which a will is validated. This means that assets like life insurance policies, retirement accounts, and annuities can be transferred swiftly and directly to the individuals you've named without the potential delays and public scrutiny that come with probate.

One of the first steps in ensuring your beneficiary designations are in order is to take stock of all your accounts, allowing such designations. These typically include your 401(k), IRA, pension plans, life insurance policies, and any other accounts with payable-on-death (POD) or transfer-on-death (TOD) features. It's a common misconception that your will has the final say over these assets. Still, the named beneficiary on each account will take precedence.

The importance of keeping your beneficiary designations current cannot be overstated. Life events such as marriage, divorce, the birth of a child, or the death of a loved one can significantly alter your intentions for your legacy. Failing to update your designations to reflect these changes can lead to unintended consequences, such as an ex-spouse receiving benefits or a newborn child being unintentionally excluded.

When selecting beneficiaries, you have the option to name primary and contingent beneficiaries. The primary beneficiary is your first choice to receive the asset. In contrast, the contingent beneficiary is your alternate choice if the primary beneficiary predeceases you or cannot inherit for any reason. This layered approach adds extra security to ensure that your assets are distributed according to your wishes.

It's also possible to name multiple beneficiaries for a single account and to specify the proportions each should receive. This can be a helpful way to divide assets among children or other heirs. However, your designations must be clear and precise to ensure clarity and clarity among your beneficiaries.

In addition to individuals, you can name trusts as beneficiaries, which can be particularly advantageous if you wish to provide for minors or individuals with special needs or if you want to impose certain conditions on the inheritance. However, this requires careful coordination with your overall estate plan to ensure that the trust's terms align with your goals and are appropriately structured to receive the designated assets.

Lastly, reviewing your beneficiary designations periodically is advisable as part of an annual financial review or whenever significant life changes occur. This practice ensures that your estate plan aligns with your current circumstances and intentions.

In summary, beneficiary designations are a powerful tool in retirement planning, offering a direct and efficient way to pass on your legacy. By thoughtfully selecting and routinely updating your beneficiaries, you can ensure that your assets are distributed according to your wishes, providing peace of mind for you and your loved ones.

Charitable Giving and Philanthropy

As you approach retirement, you've likely considered how to manage your assets and ensure they provide for your loved ones. But another aspect of estate planning can be equally fulfilling: charitable giving and philanthropy. This is not just the preserve of the ultra-wealthy; anyone can leave a philanthropic legacy that reflects their values and supports the causes they care about.

Charitable giving as part of your estate plan can take many forms, and it's essential to understand your options. One of the simplest ways to include charity in your estate plan is through a bequest in your will. You can specify a certain amount of money, a percentage of your estate, or particular assets to go to a charity of your choice. This is a straightforward way to make a significant impact, often without affecting your finances during your lifetime.

Another option is to name a charity as a beneficiary of your retirement accounts or life insurance policies. This can be an efficient way to give, as the assets typically transfer directly to the charity without going through probate. It can also have tax advantages, as the charity is tax-exempt, and the money will not be considered part of your taxable estate.

For those who wish to see their philanthropic efforts take effect during their lifetime, establishing a charitable trust might be the right choice. There are several types of charitable trusts, but they all allow you to contribute assets to a trust that will eventually benefit your chosen charity. Some, like a charitable remainder trust, can provide you or other named beneficiaries with income for some time before the remaining assets go to the charity.

Donor-advised funds (DAFs) are another popular vehicle for charitable giving. A DAF allows you to make a charitable contribution, receive an immediate tax deduction, and then recommend grants from the fund to your preferred charities over time. This can be an excellent way to involve family members in philanthropy and to create a lasting family legacy of giving.

It's also worth considering the potential tax benefits of charitable giving as part of your estate plan. Depending on how you structure your giving, you may reduce estate taxes, income taxes, or both. For example, assets given to charity are generally not subject to estate taxes, and contributions to charitable trusts or donor-advised funds may provide income tax deductions.

When incorporating charitable giving into your estate plan, working with an experienced estate planning attorney and possibly a financial advisor is crucial. They can help you understand the implications of different giving strategies and ensure that your philanthropic goals are met in a way that complements your overall estate plan.

Remember, philanthropy is deeply personal. Your charitable giving should reflect the causes and organizations you are passionate about. By thoughtfully integrating charitable strategies into your estate planning, you can create a legacy that extends beyond your lifetime and makes a lasting difference in the world.

Transferring Wealth to the Next Generation

As you approach the later stages of life, it's natural to start thinking about the legacy you'll leave behind. For many, this includes ensuring that the wealth they've accumulated over the years is passed on to the next generation in a manner that is both efficient and reflective of their wishes. Transferring wealth is not just a matter of handing over assets; it's a process that requires thoughtful planning and consideration of both financial and emotional implications.

One of the first steps in transferring wealth to your heirs is to understand what you own clearly. This includes tangible assets like property and personal belongings and intangible assets such as investments and retirement accounts. Once you have a comprehensive inventory, you must consider how each asset should be distributed. This is where a will becomes an essential tool. A will is a legal document that outlines your wishes regarding the distribution of your assets and the care of any minor children after your death.

However, a will is just one part of a larger estate plan. You'll need to designate beneficiaries for many assets, such as life insurance policies and retirement accounts. These designations are powerful, often superseding instructions in a will, so keeping them up to date and in line with your current wishes is essential.

Trusts are another critical element of estate planning that can provide greater control over how your assets are distributed. A trust can help minimize estate taxes, protect assets from creditors, and ensure that your wealth is managed according to your directives. There are various types of trusts, each with specific advantages, and choosing the right one depends on your circumstances and goals.

Taxes are an inevitable part of transferring wealth, and it's crucial to understand their impact on your estate. Estate, inheritance, and income taxes can diminish the value of the assets you leave behind if not properly managed. Working with a financial advisor or estate planner can help you develop strategies to minimize these taxes and preserve more of your wealth for your heirs.

It's also essential to have open conversations with your beneficiaries about your estate plan. Discussing your intentions can help prevent misunderstandings and conflicts after you're gone. It's an opportunity to explain your decisions, share your values, and set expectations. These conversations can be difficult but essential for a smooth wealth transition.

Finally, remember that estate planning is not a one-time task. Your life circumstances and the laws governing estate planning can change, so reviewing and updating your plan regularly is essential. This ensures that your estate plan continues to align with your current situation and that your legacy is preserved as you intend.

By taking these steps, you can create a thoughtful and effective plan for transferring wealth to the next generation, ensuring that your legacy is carried on in the way you envision.

Chapter Summary

- Estate planning is essential for controlling the distribution of assets and ensuring one's legacy is honored after death.
- It involves cataloging assets, creating a will, setting up powers of attorney, and designating beneficiaries.
- Trusts can be used for more complex estates to avoid probate, reduce taxes, and protect assets.
- Regularly updating the estate plan is crucial, especially after significant life events.
- Wills and trusts are fundamental tools in estate planning, with trusts offering benefits like avoiding probate.
- Beneficiary designations on accounts like life insurance and retirement plans are crucial as they supersede wills.
- Charitable giving can be incorporated into estate plans through bequests, trusts, or donor-advised funds, offering potential tax benefits.
- Transferring wealth to the next generation requires a precise inventory of assets, an understanding of tax implications, and open communication with heirs.

10

STAYING FINANCIALLY FIT IN RETIREMENT

Reviewing and Adjusting Your Financial Plan

Embarking on retirement is akin to setting sail on a long-anticipated voyage. You've charted your course and stocked up on provisions, and now it's time to navigate the open waters of your golden years. But just as the sea is ever-changing, so is the financial landscape of retirement. To ensure that you remain financially fit throughout this journey, reviewing and adjusting your financial plan periodically is essential.

Think of your financial plan as a living document that requires regular attention and tweaking. Life throws curveballs, and your financial strategy needs to be flexible enough to catch them. Whether it's a change in health, unexpected expenses, or shifts in the economy, your plan should be robust enough to accommodate these changes.

Start by revisiting your budget. Retirement often brings about a shift in spending patterns. Perhaps you're traveling more or have taken up new hobbies that require additional funding. Conversely, some of your anticipated expenses are lower than expected. Review your income streams and expenses at least once a year to ensure they align with your retirement goals.

Next, consider the performance of your investments. The financial markets can be volatile, and the appropriate asset allocation when you first retire might not be suitable a few years later. It's wise to assess your investment portfolio regularly with a critical eye. Are your investments providing the returns you need? Are they too risky or not risky enough? Adjustments may be necessary to strike the right balance between growth and preservation of capital.

Inflation is another factor that can erode your purchasing power over time. Your financial plan should account for a gradual increase in the cost of living. This might mean shifting some of your assets into investments that have the potential to outpace inflation, such as stocks or real estate while maintaining a portion in more stable investments like bonds or certificates of deposit for security.

Remember to review your estate plan as well. Changes in your family situation, such as marriages, divorces, births, or deaths, can have significant implications for your estate. Ensure that your will, powers of attorney, and beneficiary designations are up to date and reflect your current wishes.

Lastly, it's crucial to monitor tax laws, which can change and impact your retirement savings and income. Tax-efficient withdrawal strategies can help you keep more of your hard-earned money. Consult with a tax professional to understand the latest tax regulations and take advantage of any new tax-saving opportunities.

By regularly reviewing and adjusting your financial plan, you can stay ahead of retirement's changes. This proactive approach allows you to maintain financial fitness, ensuring that your retirement savings last as long as you do and that you can enjoy the retirement lifestyle you've worked so hard to achieve.

The Role of a Financial Advisor

As you embark on the retirement journey, one of the most significant transitions involves shifting from accumulating wealth to managing and preserving it. This is where the expertise of a financial advisor can become invaluable. A financial advisor is not just a guide; they are your partner in maintaining financial health throughout retirement.

Financial advisors bring a wealth of knowledge in investment strategies, tax laws, and estate planning, which can be complex and ever-changing. They help you navigate these waters, ensuring your retirement savings are optimized for growth and sustainability.

One of the primary responsibilities of a financial advisor is to assess your current financial situation and develop a plan that aligns with your retirement goals. This includes evaluating your income sources, such as Social Security, pensions, and investment accounts, and crafting a strategy that addresses your desired lifestyle and any unforeseen expenses.

A financial advisor will also assist in creating a withdrawal strategy that minimizes tax liabilities and maximizes the longevity of your savings. They can help determine which accounts to draw from first and how to adjust your withdrawals in response to market fluctuations and personal circumstances.

Moreover, a financial advisor can offer guidance on handling healthcare costs, often representing a significant portion of retirement expenses. They can suggest insurance options and planning techniques to protect your assets from potential long-term care costs.

Another critical aspect of a financial advisor's role is to provide a buffer against emotional decision-making. The ups and downs of the market can prompt retirees to make hasty choices that might jeopardize their financial well-being. A financial advisor offers an objective perspective, helping you stick to your long-term plan and adjust as needed without reacting to short-term market movements.

In addition to helping with financial decisions, a good financial advisor will also educate you about your investments and the rationale behind each recommendation. This empowers you to make informed decisions and fosters a sense of confidence and control over your financial future.

Lastly, a financial advisor ensures that your financial plan stays current. Life events, such as the loss of a spouse, moving to a new home, or even changes in the tax code, can all necessitate a review and potential adjustment of your financial strategy. Your advisor will be there to help you through these changes, providing the necessary advice to keep your retirement plan on track.

In summary, a financial advisor plays a multifaceted role in helping you stay financially fit in retirement. They are not only planners and strategists but also educators and confidants. With their expertise, you can feel more secure in your financial future, knowing that you have a professional looking out for your best interests as you enjoy your retirement.

Staying Informed on Economic Changes

As you transition from the working world into retirement, it's crucial to understand that staying financially fit doesn't just involve managing your savings and investments. It also requires keeping a keen eye on the broader economic landscape. The economy is dynamic and constantly in flux due to many factors, including interest rates, inflation, market trends, and global events. These changes can significantly impact your retirement funds, and being informed can help you navigate potential financial challenges.

Firstly, it's essential to recognize that economic changes can affect the purchasing power of your retirement savings. Inflation, for instance, can erode the value of money over time, meaning that what you can buy with a dollar today may differ five or ten years later. To mitigate this, you should consider investments that have the potential to outpace inflation, such as stocks or real estate, while also maintaining a portion of your portfolio in more stable assets for protection against market volatility.

Another aspect to consider is interest rates, which can influence the returns on fixed-income investments like bonds. When interest rates rise, the value of existing bonds typically falls since new bonds may be issued at higher rates, making them more attractive to investors. Conversely, when interest rates fall, existing bonds with higher rates become more valuable. Understanding these relationships can help you make more informed decisions about structuring your investment portfolio.

Keeping abreast of economic changes also means paying attention to tax laws, which can directly affect your retirement savings. Tax laws are subject to change, and new legislation can alter the landscape of retirement planning. For example, changes in tax rates or rules governing retirement account withdrawals can impact your financial strategy. Staying informed through reputable financial news sources, professional financial advisors, or educational seminars can help you anticipate and adjust to these changes.

Moreover, global economic events, such as international trade agreements or geopolitical conflicts, can also influence the markets. Diversifying your investments internationally can help spread risk and offer growth opportunities not tied to a single country's economic conditions.

In essence, staying informed on economic changes is not about reacting to every news headline or market swing. Instead, it's about solidifying how these changes can affect your retirement strategy and being prepared to make adjustments when necessary. This proactive approach can help you maintain financial fitness throughout your retirement years, ensuring your golden years remain as secure and enjoyable as possible.

Remember, the goal is not to become a financial expert overnight but to stay sufficiently informed to make wise decisions and consult with your financial advisor when needed. This approach will set the stage for continued learning and financial education, a critical component of managing your finances in retirement.

Continued Learning and Financial Education

It's crucial to understand that financial education is not a one-time event but a lifelong journey as you transition into retirement. With the basics of economic changes under your belt, it's time to focus on the importance of continued learning and financial education to stay financially fit during retirement.

Firstly, consider the financial landscape as a constantly evolving ecosystem. Just as professionals must keep up with developments in their fields, retirees should stay abreast of the latest trends in personal finance, tax laws, and investment strategies. You can still become a financial expert, but having a solid understanding of the basics can help you make informed decisions that align with your retirement goals.

One effective way to continue your financial education is by seeking out resources designed for retirees. Many community colleges and adult education programs offer retirement planning, estate planning, and investment management courses. These classes can provide valuable insights into the complexities of retirement finances and offer strategies for managing your money effectively.

Additionally, many books, online courses, and websites are dedicated to personal finance and retirement planning. Look for materials that break down complex financial concepts into digestible information. Remember, the goal is to empower yourself with knowledge, not to overwhelm yourself with jargon and intricacies best left to professionals.

Speaking of professionals, periodically consulting with a financial advisor can also be part of your continued learning. A good advisor can help you understand your current financial situation, adjust your investment portfolio as needed, and plan for future expenses. They can also serve as a sounding board for any financial ideas or concerns you may have.

Another critical aspect of continued learning is staying connected with your peers. Joining retirement groups or online forums can be an excellent way to share experiences and learn from others navigating similar financial waters. These communities often discuss managing retirement income, dealing with healthcare costs, and maximizing social security benefits.

Lastly, make it a habit to review your financial plan regularly. Your financial plan should evolve as you learn more and your circumstances change. This could mean adjusting your budget, reevaluating your risk tolerance, or exploring new investment opportunities. You can adapt to changes and maintain a comfortable lifestyle throughout retirement by staying educated and proactive about your finances.

Remember, financial fitness in retirement is not a destination but a continuous process. By committing to ongoing education and staying curious about financial matters, you can enhance your financial savvy and enjoy the peace of mind that comes with being in control of your retirement destiny.

Embracing Technology for Financial Management

In the golden years of retirement, staying financially fit isn't just about what you've saved; it's also about how you manage and monitor those savings. As we continue our journey through the essentials of retirement planning, it's time to explore technology's role in keeping your finances in top shape.

Today, technology offers many tools that can simplify financial management, making it more efficient and often more secure. Embracing these technological solutions can help you keep a close eye on your retirement funds, track spending, and stay informed about the health of your investments.

Firstly, consider the convenience of online banking. Most financial institutions now provide secure online access to your accounts, allowing you to view balances, transfer funds, and pay bills from home. This saves time and reduces the need to physically visit a bank, which can be particularly advantageous if mobility becomes an issue.

Investment tracking apps are another boon for the tech-savvy retiree. These apps can aggregate information from various investment accounts, giving you a comprehensive view of your portfolio's performance. You can monitor the ups and downs of the market, assess the balance of your asset allocation, and make informed decisions about when to buy or sell.

Budgeting software is also a critical component of financial management in retirement. These programs can help you create a budget that aligns with your fixed income, track your spending, and even forecast future expenses. By closely monitoring where your money is going, you can ensure that you're living within your means and adjust your spending habits as necessary.

For those concerned about security, technology has made great strides in protecting your financial data. Two-factor authentication, biometric logins, and encryption are security features that can help safeguard your information. It's essential to use these features where available and to stay informed about best practices for online security.

Moreover, the rise of robo-advisors has made investment advice more accessible and affordable. These automated platforms use algorithms to provide personalized investment advice based on your financial goals and risk tolerance. For retirees needing more desire or means to hire a personal financial advisor, robo-advisors can be a valuable resource for maintaining a healthy investment strategy.

Lastly, pay attention to the educational resources available online. Countless websites, webinars, and online courses can help you stay informed about financial topics relevant to retirees. Whether you want to understand the tax implications of your retirement accounts or learn about new investment opportunities, the internet is a treasure trove of information.

In conclusion, technology can be a powerful ally in managing your retirement finances. By leveraging online banking, investment tracking apps, budgeting software, and educational resources, you can clearly understand your financial health and react swiftly to any changes. Remember, staying financially fit isn't a one-time effort; it's an ongoing process that benefits greatly from modern technology's tools and conveniences.

Chapter Summary

- Regularly review and adjust your financial plan for life changes and economic shifts.

- Revisit your budget annually to align with retirement goals, considering changes in spending and income.
- Assess investment performance and adjust asset allocation to balance growth and capital preservation.
- Plan for inflation by investing in assets that can outpace it while keeping stable investments for security.
- Update your estate plan for family changes and ensure all legal documents reflect current wishes.
- Stay informed on tax laws to optimize retirement savings and income, possibly consulting a tax professional.
- A financial advisor can help manage wealth, develop tax-efficient withdrawal strategies, and provide objective advice.
- Embrace technology for efficient financial management, using online banking, investment apps, budgeting software, and staying informed through online resources.

THE GOLDEN YEARS

Lessons Learned and Wisdom Gained

As we draw the curtains on this guide to retirement planning for beginners, it's essential to pause and distill the essence of what we've learned through our exploration. The journey to retirement is as unique as the individual embarking upon it. Yet, certain universal truths have emerged that can guide us toward a fulfilling and secure retirement.

Firstly, the importance of starting early must be considered. Time is a powerful ally in compounding interest and investment growth. Those who begin their retirement savings journey when they enter the workforce, even with modest amounts, often find themselves in a much more comfortable position later in life. It's a lesson in patience and foresight—attributes that serve well beyond financial planning.

Secondly, we've learned that knowledge is a form of wealth. Understanding the basics of financial instruments, the impact of taxes, and the benefits of various retirement accounts empowers you to make informed decisions. This education should be ongoing; the financial landscape is ever-changing, and staying informed is crucial to adapt your plan to new laws, products, and economic climates.

Another lesson is the significance of living within one's means. It's a simple concept, yet it's often challenging to practice consistently. Avoiding unnecessary debt, making prudent spending choices, and prioritizing savings are habits that build a solid financial foundation, ensuring that when retirement comes, it's a time of enjoyment rather than stress.

Diversification has also emerged as a critical strategy. Putting all your eggs in one basket can be a risky endeavor. By spreading investments across different asset classes, sectors, and even geographical regions, you can mitigate risk and increase the chances of steady growth over time.

Furthermore, we've seen the value of setting clear goals and revisiting them regularly. Retirement planning isn't a set-it-and-forget-it affair. Life's milestones—marriage, children, home purchases, and career changes—can all affect your retirement goals and strategies. Regularly assessing your plan ensures it remains aligned with your evolving life circumstances.

Lastly, the wisdom of seeking professional advice cannot be understated. While having a solid grasp of retirement planning fundamentals is essential, there's no substitute for personalized advice from a financial advisor. They can provide insights tailored to your situation, helping you navigate complex decisions and optimize your retirement plan.

As we move forward, let's carry these lessons with us. They are the building blocks for a retirement that's not only financially secure but also rich in the experiences and joys of having the freedom and peace of mind to enjoy your golden years truly.

The Importance of Flexibility and Adaptability

As we embrace the golden years of retirement, it's essential to understand that the journey is not only about the plans we've meticulously crafted but also about our ability to adapt to the unexpected twists and turns life may present. Flexibility and adaptability become critical components in ensuring that our retirement years are secure and fulfilling.

We often follow a structured path with clear goals and timelines throughout our working lives. However, retirement introduces a new level of freedom coupled with uncertainty. The stock market may fluctuate, health may change, and personal relationships may evolve—all factors impacting our retirement experience. It's here that being flexible with our plans and adaptable to change can make a significant difference.

Consider the financial aspect: a fixed-income portfolio that seemed perfect at the onset of retirement might need adjustments as economic conditions change. Being open to revisiting and revising your investment strategies can help safeguard your nest egg against inflation and market volatility. Similarly, healthcare needs often become more complex as we age. Staying informed about Medicare options and supplemental insurance plans and being willing to adjust coverage as health needs can prevent unexpected medical expenses from derailing your financial security.

On a more personal level, adaptability plays a crucial role in maintaining a vibrant social life and finding new passions. The activities and hobbies that excite you at the beginning of retirement may shift over time. Being open to exploring new interests, joining different community groups, or even relocating to a more retiree-friendly environment can enhance your quality of life.

Moreover, flexibility in your daily routine can lead to unexpected joys. You may discover a love for volunteering, mentoring, or part-time work in a field you've always been passionate about. These activities can structure your days while allowing you the freedom to set your own pace.

In essence, the golden years of retirement are not just a

period to enjoy the fruits of your labor but also a time for growth and adaptation. By staying flexible in your plans and adaptable to the changing tides of life, you can navigate the uncertainties of retirement with confidence and grace. This approach ensures a more resilient financial standing and enriches your life with new experiences and opportunities for personal development.

As we move forward, the lessons we've learned and the wisdom we've gained become the legacy we pass on. It's not just about the assets we leave behind but also the example we set on how to live a whole and adaptable life in retirement.

Passing on Your Legacy

As you approach the twilight of your golden years, the concept of legacy becomes increasingly significant. Retirement planning is not just about ensuring you have the financial means to live comfortably; it's also about the mark you leave on the world and how you touch the lives of those you care about. Passing on your legacy is a multifaceted process that encompasses the tangible assets you've accumulated over a lifetime and the values, lessons, and memories you wish to bestow upon future generations.

Your legacy is the lasting impression you make, culminating in your life's work, beliefs, and the love you share. It's the stories your family recounts at gatherings, the wisdom you've imparted to your children and grandchildren, and your impact on your community. As you consider how you want to be remembered, consider how you can actively shape your legacy.

One practical step in passing on your legacy is to ensure your financial affairs are in order. This includes having an up-to-date will, considering trusts for asset protection, and making clear designations for beneficiaries on your financial accounts and insurance policies. It's also prudent to have conversations with your loved ones about your end-of-life wishes, including any medical directives or preferences for memorial services.

Beyond the financial aspect, consider writing a personal letter or recording a video message that shares your life stories, values, and hopes for your family's future. This can be an invaluable gift, providing comfort and guidance even when you're no longer physically present.

Engaging in philanthropy or charitable giving can also be a part of your legacy. Whether through regular donations, volunteering, or setting up a scholarship fund, these acts of kindness can carry your influence forward and reflect the causes you hold dear.

Remember, your legacy is not just about what you leave behind; it's also about how you live today. Continue to nurture relationships, invest in the growth of others, and contribute positively to your community. These actions will resonate and form the foundation of the legacy you pass on.

In the end, your legacy is a bridge between the past, present, and future. It's a way to ensure that your life's journey continues to inspire and guide those who follow in your footsteps. As you reflect on the legacy you wish to create, know it's always possible to make meaningful contributions that will echo through the generations.

Looking Ahead: Continuous Growth and Enjoyment

As we turn the page from considering the legacy we wish to leave behind, it's equally important to focus on our retirement years' present and future aspects. Retirement isn't a final destination; it's a new chapter that offers continuous growth and enjoyment. The key to a fulfilling retirement is to embrace this period as an opportunity for personal development and to find joy in the everyday.

Firstly, let's talk about growth. Retirement is the perfect time to explore interests you may have put on hold during your working years. Whether learning a new language, picking up a musical instrument, or diving into gardening, these activities are not just hobbies but avenues for mental stimulation and skill development. Lifelong learning keeps the mind sharp and can lead to a more satisfying retirement. Many community colleges and universities offer courses specifically designed for retirees, and online platforms provide endless opportunities to learn at your own pace.

In addition to intellectual growth, physical activity is paramount. Regular exercise can help manage health issues, improve mood, and increase social interaction. Joining a local walking group, signing up for dance classes, or simply dedicating time each day for a swim can significantly impact your overall well-being. Remember, it's not about intensity but consistency and finding an activity you enjoy.

Social engagement is another critical component of a rewarding retirement. Maintaining old friendships and building new ones can prevent feelings of isolation and provide a support network. Consider volunteer work, joining clubs, or participating in community events to stay connected with others. Social interactions can also provide a sense of purpose and belonging, which is essential for happiness at any age.

Financial health continues to be a priority, even after the initial stages of retirement planning. Reviewing your financial situation regularly is essential to ensure your savings and investments align with your current needs and future goals. This may involve adjusting your budget to accommodate changes in your lifestyle or consulting with a financial advisor to discuss any concerns.

Lastly, remember to savor the small moments that bring joy. Whether it's a morning cup of coffee on the porch, an afternoon spent with grandchildren, or an evening of stargazing, these simple pleasures can provide profound happiness. Retirement offers the luxury of time filled with the things that matter most to you.

In conclusion, your golden years can be just that—golden—if approached with a mindset geared towards continuous growth and enjoyment. By engaging in lifelong learning, staying physically active, maintaining social connections, managing your finances, and appreciating life's simple joys, you can craft a fulfilling and dynamic retirement. As we close this chapter on retirement planning, remember that your retirement story is one you continue to write daily with every choice and new adventure.

ESTATE PLANNING FOR BEGINNERS

A COMPREHENSIVE GUIDE TO ASSET
PROTECTION, BENEFICIARY
MANAGEMENT, AND SECURING YOUR
LEGACY

INTRODUCTION TO ESTATE PLANNING

What is Estate Planning?

Estate planning might evoke images of grand mansions and vast fortunes, but it's not just for the wealthy. It's a process that allows anyone, regardless of their financial status, to set out instructions for managing and distributing their assets after they pass away. It also encompasses decisions about your healthcare and financial affairs should you become unable to make them yourself.

At its core, estate planning is about ensuring that your wishes are honored, your loved ones are provided for, and your legacy is preserved according to your design, not left to the state's default rules. It's a comprehensive approach that includes drafting legal documents like wills, trusts, powers of attorney, and healthcare directives. Each serves a specific purpose, from designating heirs and beneficiaries to appoint someone to decide on your behalf if you're incapacitated.

Estate planning is not a one-time event but an ongoing process. Your estate plan should evolve as life changes— marriages, divorces, births, deaths, and changes in the law. It's about maintaining control over your affairs, protecting your assets, and providing peace of mind for you and those you care about.

By creating a thoughtful estate plan, you can avoid leaving your heirs with the potential burden of probate, minimize taxes and legal fees, and prevent family disputes. It's a way to ensure that your story—your values, care for your family, and charitable inclinations—is told how you want it to be.

Essentially, estate planning is a deeply personal yet universally important process. It's about making clear and legally recognized decisions that reflect your wishes and protect your most cherished assets—your family and your legacy.

The Importance of Estate Planning

Having explored the basics of estate planning, it's crucial to understand why dedicating time and resources to this process is beneficial and essential. At its core, estate planning is about securing peace of mind for yourself and ensuring that your loved ones are provided for in your absence. It's a proactive approach to managing your assets and legacy, essential for several reasons.

Firstly, estate planning allows you to maintain control over your assets. Without a plan, state laws determine how your assets are distributed after passing. This may not align with your wishes or the needs of your beneficiaries. Creating an estate plan ensures that your assets go exactly where you want them to—to family, friends, or charitable organizations.

Secondly, estate planning can significantly reduce the stress and burden on your family during a difficult time. The loss of a loved one is an emotional ordeal, and the added pressure of sorting out financial and legal matters can be overwhelming. An estate plan provides clear instructions on handling your affairs, which can alleviate potential conflicts and confusion among your heirs.

Another important aspect of estate planning is the potential to minimize taxes and other expenses. With the right strategies in place, you can reduce the amount of your estate that goes to taxes, legal fees, and court costs, thereby maximizing the value of the inheritance you leave behind.

Furthermore, estate planning is not only about the distribution of assets; it also encompasses decisions about your care should you become incapacitated. Through powers of attorney and healthcare directives, you can appoint someone you trust to manage your finances and make medical decisions if you cannot.

Lastly, estate planning is an ongoing process. Life changes—such as marriage, divorce, the birth of children, and the acquisition of new assets—mean your estate plan should evolve to reflect your current circumstances and goals. Regularly reviewing and updating your plan ensures it remains effective and aligned with your intentions.

Essentially, estate planning is a fundamental step in managing your personal affairs. It's about taking charge of your future, protecting your assets, and caring for the people you love. With the right plan, you can leave a lasting, positive impact beyond your lifetime.

Common Misconceptions

As we delve into estate planning, clearing the fog of misconceptions surrounding this critical process is crucial. Many people approach estate planning with preconceived notions that may hinder their ability to plan effectively for the future. Let's dispel some of these myths to set a solid foundation for your understanding.

Firstly, there's a common belief that estate planning is only for the wealthy. This couldn't be further from the truth. Regardless of the size of your assets, estate planning is about ensuring that what you own is transferred according to your wishes and in the most efficient manner possible. It's about protecting your loved ones and ensuring that unnecessary taxes or legal fees do not erode the fruits of your labor.

Another widespread misconception is that estate planning solely distributes assets after death. A comprehensive estate plan also addresses your needs while you're alive. It includes directives for managing your finances and healthcare decisions if you need help to do so yourself. Often overlooked, this aspect of estate planning is as vital as planning for asset distribution.

Many beginners also mistakenly think that once an estate plan is created, it's set in stone. The truth is that estate planning is an ongoing process. Life changes—such as marriage, divorce, the birth of a child, or the acquisition of new assets—necessitate updates to your estate plan to reflect your current situation and wishes.

Lastly, there's the myth that estate planning is too complex and expensive for the average person. While it's true that estate planning can be complex, it doesn't have to be prohibitively expensive. With the proper guidance and a step-by-step approach, you can create an estate plan that fits your needs without breaking the bank.

Understanding these misconceptions is the first step in recognizing the true nature and scope of estate planning. It's a process that is as personal as it is critical and accessible to everyone. With these myths out of the way, we can focus on the actual goals of estate planning, which will help you secure your legacy and provide for your loved ones in the best way possible.

Goals of Estate Planning

Having dispelled some common misconceptions about estate planning, we must focus on the core objectives that make this process so critical for individuals and families. At its essence, estate planning is a proactive approach to organizing your personal and financial affairs. The goals of estate planning are both varied and personal, but they typically include the following key objectives:

- **Distribution of Assets:** One of the primary goals of estate planning is to ensure that your assets are distributed according to your wishes after you pass away. Without a plan, state laws will determine how your assets are divided, which might not align with your preferences. A well-crafted estate plan allows you to designate beneficiaries for your assets, which can include family members, friends, or charitable organizations.
- **Protection of Loved Ones:** Estate planning is about assets and ensuring your loved ones are provided for and protected. This can mean setting up trusts for minor children or dependents with special needs, choosing guardians, or ensuring that a surviving spouse is financially secure.
- **Minimizing Taxes and Expenses:** A thoughtful estate plan can help minimize taxes, court costs, and legal fees. Utilizing various estate planning tools, such as trusts, you can reduce the estate tax burden on your heirs and preserve more of your estate for their benefit.
- **Avoiding Probate:** Probate is the legal process through which a deceased person's estate is properly distributed to heirs and designated beneficiaries, and any debt owed to creditors is paid off. It can be time-consuming and expensive. Many people aim to avoid probate through their estate planning efforts to expedite the distribution of their assets and reduce costs.

- **Planning for Incapacity:** Estate planning also addresses the possibility of your becoming incapacitated before death. Through powers of attorney and living wills, you can appoint someone to manage your financial affairs, make healthcare decisions, and communicate your wishes regarding life-sustaining treatment if you cannot do so yourself.
- **Charitable Intentions:** If you have philanthropic goals, estate planning can help you establish a legacy of giving. You can set up charitable trusts or make specific bequests in your will to support the causes and organizations that are important to you.
- **Business Succession:** For business owners, estate planning is crucial for the continuation or orderly succession of the business. It involves planning for the transition of ownership and management to ensure the business continues to operate smoothly without you.
- **Peace of Mind:** Finally, one of the most significant goals of estate planning is to provide peace of mind for you and your loved ones. Knowing that you have a plan articulating your wishes can alleviate stress and potential conflicts among those you leave behind.

As we move forward, we will delve into the estate planning process, providing a roadmap for creating a comprehensive plan that aligns with these goals. The process involves several steps, from taking inventory of your assets to executing the necessary legal documents, and each step is designed to help you achieve a secure and intentional plan for your legacy.

Overview of the Estate Planning Process

Having established the fundamental goals of estate planning in the previous section, it's time to delve into the estate planning process. This journey is not just about drafting documents; it's about creating a roadmap for the future that reflects your wishes and provides for your loved ones. The process can be intricate, but it becomes manageable and less daunting with a step-by-step approach.

Firstly, let's begin with taking stock of your assets. This includes everything you own—real estate, bank accounts, investments, retirement funds, insurance policies, and personal property. Having a clear picture of what you have is essential because this will form the basis of your estate plan.

Next, consider your beneficiaries. These are the people or entities you want to inherit your assets. You are deciding who gets what, which is a personal decision that should be made carefully. It's also essential to consider alternate beneficiaries if your primary choices cannot be inherited.

Once you've identified your assets and beneficiaries, it's time to think about how you want to distribute your assets. This involves making decisions about who gets what and when. For example, you might want some beneficiaries to receive their inheritance outright. In contrast, others might receive theirs through a trust that provides for more controlled distribution.

Another critical component is selecting fiduciaries—individuals you trust to fulfill your wishes. This includes an executor of your will, a trustee if you establish a trust, and agents for financial and healthcare powers of attorney. These roles are pivotal, as these people will be responsible for managing your estate and making decisions on your behalf if you cannot do so.

With these decisions in mind, it's time to create the legal documents to ensure your wishes are honored. The most common documents in an estate plan include a will, a durable power of attorney for finances, a healthcare power of attorney, and often a trust. Each serves a unique purpose and works together to form a comprehensive estate plan.

After drafting these documents, reviewing them regularly and updating them as your life circumstances change is crucial. Marriage, divorce, the birth of children or grandchildren, and significant changes in financial status are all events that should trigger a review of your estate plan.

Lastly, it's essential to communicate your plans to your loved ones. While it might be a difficult conversation, it's essential to ensure that your wishes are understood and that your family knows where to find your important documents when the time comes.

Remember, estate planning is not a one-time event but an ongoing process. As your life evolves, so too should your estate plan. By taking these steps, you can create a plan that provides peace of mind for you and security for your beneficiaries.

Chapter Summary

- Estate planning is for everyone, not just the wealthy, and involves managing assets and healthcare decisions.
- It includes creating wills, trusts, powers of attorney, and healthcare directives, and it should be updated with life changes.
- Estate planning ensures assets are distributed as desired, reduces family stress, minimizes taxes, and plans for incapacity.
- Common misconceptions include that it's only for the rich, it's only about death, it's set in stone, and it's too complex or expensive.

- Goals include asset distribution, protecting loved ones, minimizing taxes, avoiding probate, planning for incapacity, charitable giving, business succession, and peace of mind.
- The process involves inventorying assets, choosing beneficiaries, deciding asset distribution, selecting fiduciaries, and creating legal documents.
- Regular updates to the estate plan are necessary due to life changes, and communication with loved ones is crucial.
- Estate planning is an ongoing process that evolves with life's changes, providing security and peace of mind.

1

UNDERSTANDING YOUR ASSETS

Identifying Your Assets

Embarking on the estate planning journey can often feel like you're trying to navigate a maze without a map. But fear not! The first step to finding your path is identifying what you're bringing along for the journey—your assets. In this section, we'll explore the various types of assets you may have and how to compile a comprehensive list that will serve as the cornerstone of your estate plan.

Think of your assets as the building blocks of your financial life. They are the tangible and intangible items you own that have value. You'll want to create a clear and detailed inventory to get started. This list should be thorough, as it will be crucial for the next steps in your estate planning process.

Begin with the most apparent items: your real estate. This includes your home, vacation properties, rental properties, or land you own. Next, consider your personal property, including vehicles, jewelry, art, collectibles, and furniture. You can touch and feel these items, and they often carry both sentimental and monetary value.

Moving on to financial assets, this category includes the contents of your bank accounts—checking, savings, and certificates of deposit. It also covers investments like stocks, bonds, mutual funds, and retirement accounts such as IRAs and 401(k)s. Don't overlook life insurance policies and annuities, which can be significant financial resources for your beneficiaries.

Business owners will need to include their business interests. Whether you own a small family business or a share of a larger enterprise, these interests are a vital part of your asset portfolio.

Lastly, consider any intellectual property you own, such as patents, copyrights, or trademarks. These can be valuable assets, especially if they generate ongoing royalties or have the potential for future monetization.

As you compile this list, remember to include digital assets as well. In our increasingly online world, these can range from social media accounts to cryptocurrency holdings and even domain names you own.

Once you have a comprehensive list, you'll have a clearer picture of what you own—a crucial step before you can effectively plan for how these assets will be managed during your life and distributed after your passing. With this inventory in hand, you'll be ready to move on to the next phase: valuing your assets, which is essential for understanding the potential tax implications and making informed decisions about your estate.

Valuing Your Assets

Now that you've identified your assets, the next crucial phase in estate planning is understanding their value. Valuing your assets is not just about knowing their current market price; it's about recognizing the economic worth they hold for you and your beneficiaries. This valuation will serve as a cornerstone for various decisions in your estate planning journey, including tax planning, distribution of assets, and ensuring your loved ones are taken care of according to your wishes.

To begin with, let's consider liquid assets. These are the assets that can be easily converted into cash. Examples include savings accounts, stocks, bonds, and mutual funds. The value of these assets is generally straightforward to determine. You can look at your latest account statements or check the current market prices for stocks and bonds. Keeping these valuations current is essential, as they can fluctuate with market conditions.

Next, we have real estate, which includes your home, any rental properties, or land you own. Valuing real estate can be more complex due to location, condition, market trends, and property improvements. Consider consulting with a professional appraiser or looking at recent sales of comparable properties in your area for an accurate assessment.

Personal property, such as vehicles, jewelry, art, and collectibles, must also be valued. Resources like Kelley Blue Book can reasonably estimate everyday items like cars. However, for items like art or antiques, you might need a professional appraisal to understand their market value, especially if they are rare or have historical significance.

Business interests present another layer of complexity. Determining its value can be intricate if you own a business or a share of one. It may involve analyzing the company's financial statements, considering its earning potential, and obtaining a professional business valuation.

Retirement accounts, including IRAs and 401(k)s, are valued based on the current statements provided by the financial institutions managing these accounts. Remember that these types of accounts may have tax implications that affect their value to your beneficiaries.

Lastly, life insurance policies are unique assets. Their value to your estate is not the cash surrender value but the death benefit your beneficiaries will receive. This amount should be considered in the overall valuation of your assets, as it can significantly impact your estate's liquidity upon your passing.

In valuing your assets, it's also essential to consider any debts or liabilities against them, as these will affect the net value of your estate. Mortgages, loans, and credit card debts must be subtracted from the asset values to get a clear picture of your net worth.

Remember, valuing your assets is not a one-time task. It's a dynamic process that should be revisited regularly or when significant life events occur. Keeping your asset valuations current will ensure that your estate plan remains relevant and practical, reflecting your actual financial situation at any given time.

By understanding the value of your assets, you are better equipped to make informed decisions about how to structure your estate plan. This clarity will help you in the following steps, where you'll consider the implications of different types of ownership and how they can affect the transfer of your assets.

Types of Ownership

In estate planning, understanding the types of ownership tied to your assets is as crucial as knowing their value. Ownership dictates who can use, manage, and ultimately inherit these assets, so it's essential to grasp the different forms of ownership and how they may affect your estate plan.

To start, let's talk about sole ownership. This is the simplest form: if you own an asset in your name alone, you have complete control over it. This includes the right to sell, gift, or bequeath the asset as you see fit. Common examples of sole ownership include personal items, a car, or a bank account that doesn't have a designated beneficiary or co-owner.

Next, joint ownership involves sharing control of an asset with one or more individuals. The most common type of joint ownership is joint tenancy with right of survivorship. If one owner passes away, their asset share automatically passes to the surviving owner(s), bypassing the probate process. This is often used for real estate, bank accounts, and other significant assets.

Another form of joint ownership is tenancy in common, where each owner has a distinct, divisible interest in the asset. Unlike joint tenancy, there's no right of survivorship; when one owner dies, their share becomes part of their estate and is distributed according to their will or state law if there's no will.

For married couples, some states recognize tenancy by the entirety, which is similar to joint tenancy but adds a layer of protection against creditors and allows ownership to transfer seamlessly to the surviving spouse.

Then there's community property, a concept that applies in some states, primarily in the western United States. In these jurisdictions, assets acquired during a marriage are considered jointly owned by both spouses, regardless of whose name is on the title. This can significantly affect estate planning, as each spouse claims half of the community property.

Understanding the nuances of these ownership types is more than just academic; it directly impacts how you plan for the future of your assets. For instance, assets owned jointly with the right of survivorship will not be part of your probate estate so that they won't be distributed according to your will. This can be a blessing and a potential source of conflict if it's different from what you intended.

Considering these ownership types, it's also important to recognize that designations like beneficiaries on life insurance policies and retirement accounts can override what's written in your will. These designations are a form of "payable on death" ownership, where the asset passes directly to the named beneficiary.

In the digital age, it's also vital to consider the ownership of digital assets, which can include everything from social media accounts to digital currencies. But we'll delve deeper into that topic in the next section.

For now, take stock of your assets and consider their value and how they're owned. This will guide how you structure your estate plan to ensure that your assets are distributed according to your wishes and that the process is as smooth and conflict-free as possible for your heirs.

Digital Assets

In the digital age, your estate is no longer limited to tangible assets like real estate, vehicles, or family heirlooms. A significant and often overlooked component of modern estate planning is the management of digital assets. These are the electronic records and files you own or control, and they can range from the sentimental to the financially significant.

To begin with, consider your digital assets. These may include digital photographs, videos, social media accounts, and personal emails. While they might not hold monetary value, they are often rich in sentimental value and an integral part of your digital legacy. Deciding what should happen to these personal digital assets after you pass away is an essential step in estate planning. You should designate a digital executor, someone you trust to handle your digital presence according to your wishes.

Next, there are digital assets with clear financial value. These could be your online banking accounts, investment portfolios, and cryptocurrency holdings. As you would with traditional financial assets, ensuring that your beneficiaries have the necessary information to access these digital funds is crucial. However, unlike traditional assets, digital ones may require specific usernames, passwords, and even two-factor authentication methods to access.

Moreover, you may own digital business assets if you're an entrepreneur or involved in online business activities. These include domain names, online stores, blogs, and associated revenue streams. These assets can be significant and may require special consideration to transfer ownership or control as part of your estate.

Intellectual property in digital form, such as ebooks, digital music, and software you've created, also falls under this category. These assets can continue to generate income beyond your lifetime, so it's essential to establish who will control and benefit from them.

When planning for your digital assets, compiling a comprehensive inventory is essential. This list should include details such as the type of asset, where it's located, and how to access it. Remember, laws governing access to digital assets after someone's death are still evolving. Hence, it's wise to consult an estate planning attorney knowledgeable about the digital realm.

Lastly, be aware of the terms of service agreements for your online accounts. Some platforms have specific policies for handling accounts after a user's death, which can affect how you plan for these assets.

By managing your digital assets, you ensure that your online life is as organized and respected as your physical one, providing peace of mind for you and clarity for your loved ones.

Business Interests

In the realm of estate planning, understanding the full scope of your assets is crucial. Among these assets, business interests often stand out as valuable and complex. Suppose you're an entrepreneur or a stakeholder in a business. In that case, these interests can form a significant part of your estate and require careful consideration to ensure they are managed according to your wishes after you pass away.

Business interests can range from sole proprietorships and partnerships to shares in a corporation or membership interests in a limited liability company (LLC). Each type of business interest has its own set of rules for succession and transferability, which company bylaws, shareholder agreements, and state laws can influence.

The business and the owner are legally considered one and the same for sole proprietorships. This means that the business does not continue to exist as a separate entity upon the owner's death. Instead, its assets and liabilities become part of the owner's estate. They are distributed according to their will or state intestacy laws if no will exists.

In the case of partnerships, the situation can be more complex. Unless a partnership agreement specifies what happens when a partner dies, the partnership may automatically dissolve. To prevent this, partners often have buy-sell agreements in place, which allow the surviving partners to purchase the deceased partner's interest, providing liquidity to the estate and continuity for the business.

For those with interests in corporations, mainly closely held corporations, the transfer of shares after death can be governed by shareholder agreements. These agreements often include provisions restricting the transfer of shares to maintain control within a particular group, such as family members or existing shareholders. They may also outline buy-sell provisions similar to those in partnerships.

Suppose you have an ownership stake in an LLC. In that case, the operating agreement is the crucial document that will dictate what happens to your membership interest upon your death. It's essential to review and understand the terms of the operating agreement, as they can vary widely from one LLC to another. Some may allow the interest to pass to heirs, while others may require that the interest be sold back to the LLC or the remaining members.

Regardless of your business interest, it's essential to have a clear succession plan in place. This plan should address who will take over the management of the business, how ownership interests will be transferred, and how the value of your business interests will be determined. It's also wise to consider the potential tax implications of transferring business interests, as they can be significant.

To ensure that your business interests are handled according to your wishes, it's advisable to work with an estate planning attorney who has experience with business succession planning. They can help you navigate the complexities of transferring business interests and integrate these plans into your overall estate strategy.

Remember, your business is a legacy that can provide for your family or chosen successors long after you're gone. With thoughtful planning, you can ensure that this legacy is preserved and that the transition of your business interests is as smooth and beneficial as possible for those you leave behind.

Chapter Summary

- Begin estate planning by identifying and listing all assets, including real estate, personal property, financial assets, business interests, and intellectual property.
- Include digital assets such as social media accounts and cryptocurrency in the inventory.
- Value assets by considering current market prices and professional appraisals and account for any debts against them.
- Regularly update asset valuations to reflect changes in market conditions or personal circumstances.
- Understand different types of asset ownership, such as sole ownership, joint tenancy, tenancy in common, and community property.
- Recognize that ownership types and beneficiary designations affect asset distribution after death.
- Manage digital assets by creating an inventory and providing access information while considering online platform policies.
- For business interests, understand succession and transfer rules, create a clear plan, and consult an estate planning attorney.

2

YOUR BENEFICIARIES

Defining Your Beneficiaries

Regarding estate planning, determining your beneficiaries is one of the most crucial steps. You designate these individuals or entities to receive your assets upon your passing. It's a decision that requires careful thought and clear articulation to ensure your wishes are fulfilled as intended.

Beneficiaries include family members, friends, charitable organizations, or pets. They can be primary beneficiaries, who are first in line to receive your assets, or contingent beneficiaries, who will receive your assets if the primary beneficiaries cannot do so.

To define your beneficiaries, you'll need to consider the nature of your relationships and the needs of each potential recipient. For example, you can provide for your spouse or domestic partner, children, siblings, or aging parents. It's also important to consider the financial implications for your beneficiaries, such as any potential tax burdens that your legacy might impose on them.

When selecting beneficiaries, be as specific as possible to avoid any ambiguity. Instead of simply stating "my children" as beneficiaries, list their full names and other identifying information to clarify your intentions. This specificity is crucial to prevent disputes among family members and ensure your assets are distributed according to your wishes.

It's also wise to review and update your beneficiary designations periodically, especially after significant life events such as marriage, divorce, the birth of a child, or the death of a loved one. Life changes can have significant implications for your estate plan, and keeping your beneficiary designations current will help to avoid unintended consequences.

Remember, your choices regarding your beneficiaries will have a lasting impact. Take the time to reflect on your relationships and the needs of those you care about. Consider speaking with an estate planning attorney who can provide guidance tailored to your unique circumstances and help you navigate the complexities of beneficiary designations. With careful planning and clear communication, you can create a legacy that reflects your values and intentions.

Special Considerations for Minor Children

As you embark on the estate planning journey, one of the most heartfelt considerations is the well-being of your minor children. It's natural to want to ensure they are cared for and financially secure in your absence. However, leaving assets directly to children under the legal age of majority—typically 18 or 21, depending on your state—can complicate matters. Let's navigate these waters together to ensure your intentions for your children's future are met with care and legal prudence.

Firstly, it's essential to understand that minors cannot legally own substantial property in their names. Suppose you pass away, leaving assets directly to a minor without any legal arrangements. In that case, the court will appoint a guardian to manage those assets until the child reaches adulthood. This process can be time-consuming and expensive and may result in something other than your chosen person.

To avoid these complications, consider establishing a trust for your minor children. A trust lets you set terms for how and when the assets will be distributed. You can appoint a trustee whom you trust to manage the assets according to your instructions. This could include stipulations for education expenses, health care, living costs, and even distributions at certain ages or milestones.

Another option is to use the Uniform Transfers to Minors Act (UTMA) or Uniform Gifts to Minors Act (UGMA) accounts. These accounts allow you to transfer assets to a custodian who will manage them for the benefit of the minor until they reach a certain age—often 18 or 21. While more straightforward than a trust, these accounts offer less control over how the funds are used once the child reaches the age of majority.

Life insurance policies also require special consideration. Suppose you name your minor children as beneficiaries. In that case, the proceeds may be subject to the same issues as other assets left directly to them. Instead, you can name a trust as the policy's beneficiary, ensuring the proceeds are managed according to your terms.

Lastly, it's crucial to select a guardian for your minor children in your will. If you're not there, this person will care for your children's daily needs. While this decision is deeply personal and challenging, it's one of the most significant acts of love. It cares you can provide for your children.

Remember, the goal of estate planning is not just to pass on what you own but to pass on your values and provide for your loved ones according to your wishes. By considering these special considerations for your minor children, you're creating a framework that supports their growth and well-being, even when you're not there to guide them.

When Beneficiaries Have Special Needs

When planning your estate, it's crucial to consider the unique needs of any beneficiaries with disabilities or special needs. This consideration is not just a matter of sensitivity; it's about ensuring that the support you provide through your estate doesn't inadvertently disqualify them from essential government benefits or services they may receive.

Firstly, understand that direct inheritance can sometimes do more harm than good. For instance, if a beneficiary with special needs receives Supplemental Security Income (SSI) or Medicaid, an inheritance could increase their assets to a level that exceeds eligibility thresholds. This could result in a loss of benefits that are critical to their well-being.

To navigate this, many turn to a tool known as a Special Needs Trust (SNT). This type of trust allows you to leave assets for the benefit of a person with special needs without those assets being counted against them for eligibility purposes. The trust is managed by a trustee who disburses funds to cover costs that government benefits do not, such as personal care attendants, out-of-pocket medical expenses, or education services.

When setting up an SNT, it's essential to choose a trustworthy and knowledgeable trustee who is aware of the beneficiary's needs and government benefits rules. This person will have significant discretion over the trust's assets and must be able to manage them in a way that continues to protect the beneficiary's eligibility for aid.

Another consideration is the use of a letter of intent. While not legally binding, this document provides a detailed overview of the beneficiary's preferences, routines, medical needs, and other important information. It guides trustees and future caregivers to ensure the beneficiary's quality of life is maintained according to your wishes.

Lastly, updating your estate plan is essential as laws and circumstances change. Regular reviews with an attorney specializing in special needs planning can help ensure that your estate plan continues to serve the best interests of your beneficiaries with special needs.

Remember, thoughtful planning is the cornerstone of providing for a special-needs beneficiary. It's not just about the assets you leave behind but also about the structures and guidance you put in place to ensure those assets improve the quality of life for your loved ones without unintended consequences.

Managing Potential Conflicts Among Beneficiaries

Estate planning is not just about ensuring your assets are distributed according to your wishes; it's also about maintaining harmony among those you leave behind. As we delve into managing potential conflicts among beneficiaries, we must remember that emotions can run high regarding inheritance matters. Taking proactive steps can minimize disputes and ensure your legacy is peaceful rather than discord.

Firstly, clear communication is critical. It's advisable to discuss your estate plan with your beneficiaries while you can. This doesn't mean you need to divulge every detail, but explaining the reasoning behind your decisions can help prevent misunderstandings later on. If you've made unequal distributions, for instance, explaining that you've done so because one child has a greater financial need or has already provided substantial support to another can help mitigate feelings of favoritism or neglect.

Secondly, consider using a no-contest clause in your will or trust. This clause states that if a beneficiary challenges the estate plan and loses, they will receive nothing. While this can be a powerful deterrent to legal battles, it could be more foolproof and sometimes fuel the fire if beneficiaries feel coerced. It's essential to weigh the pros and cons of such a clause and to consult with an estate planning attorney to determine its effectiveness and legality in your jurisdiction.

Another strategy is to appoint an impartial executor or trustee. This should be someone who is not a beneficiary and can manage your estate objectively. The role of the executor is to administer your estate according to your wishes, and having someone who does not have a personal stake in the outcome can reduce the potential for conflict.

Additionally, consider creating a personal property memorandum. This document outlines who should receive specific items of sentimental or monetary value. It can be updated easily without changing your will or trust, allowing you to adapt to changing circumstances or relationships. By being specific about who gets what, you can avoid disputes over personal belongings, often the source of significant conflict among heirs.

Lastly, setting up a trust can be wise for those with significant assets. Trusts can provide a structured way to distribute your assets over time, which can be particularly helpful if you're concerned about a beneficiary's spending habits or want to provide for them in a way that doesn't involve a lump sum. Trusts can also offer privacy and avoid the probate process, which can be lengthy and contentious.

In conclusion, while it's impossible to predict every outcome, taking these steps can go a long way in preventing conflicts among your beneficiaries. By being thoughtful and thorough in your estate planning, you can help ensure that your legacy is preserved and that your loved ones are provided for in a way that promotes harmony rather than discord. Remember, the ultimate goal is to provide for your beneficiaries in a manner that aligns with your values and wishes while also considering their individual needs and relationships with one another.

Charitable Bequests

After ensuring that your loved ones are cared for in estate planning, consider leaving a lasting legacy through charitable bequests. This is a way to support causes and organizations close to your heart, even after you're gone.

Charitable bequests are gifts made as part of your will or trust that designate a portion of your estate to a charity or nonprofit organization. These gifts can take various forms, such as a specific dollar amount, a percentage of your estate, or particular assets. They can also be contingent upon certain conditions being met, such as the survival of other beneficiaries.

One of the primary benefits of including charitable bequests in your estate plan is the potential for tax relief. Charitable gifts can reduce the value of your estate for estate tax purposes, which can be significant if your estate exceeds the federal estate tax exemption amount. Additionally, if you have a taxable estate, these endowments can reduce or even eliminate the estate tax liability.

When selecting a charity for a legacy, it's essential to do your due diligence. Ensure that the organization is a qualified 501(c)(3) charity, which means that the IRS has recognized it as a tax-exempt organization. This status is crucial for the tax benefits of your legacy to be realized. You can verify an organization's status through the IRS website or request a copy of their determination letter.

It's also wise to be specific in your will or trust about which charity you want to benefit and how you want the funds to be used. If you have a particular program or purpose, stipulate this in your estate documents. This can help prevent ambiguity and ensure your charitable goals are met.

Discuss your intentions with the charity beforehand if you consider a significant gift. Many organizations have planned giving departments that can work with you to ensure your bequest is used according to your wishes. They can also provide specific language to include in your will or trust to facilitate the gift.

Remember, charitable bequests are not just for the wealthy. Even modest gifts can substantially impact an organization and its work. Plus, giving charitably can set a powerful example for your heirs, inspiring them to continue a legacy of generosity.

In conclusion, charitable bequests are a meaningful way to extend your influence and values beyond your lifetime. By thoughtfully integrating these gifts into your estate plan, you can support the causes you care about while reaping potential tax benefits and shaping how you are remembered. As with all aspects of estate planning, consulting with an estate planning attorney is advisable to ensure that your charitable intentions are clearly articulated and legally sound.

Chapter Summary

- Estate planning involves carefully choosing beneficiaries, such as family, friends, charities, or pets, to receive assets after one's passing.
- Beneficiaries can be primary or contingent; specificity in naming them helps avoid disputes and ensures wishes are followed.
- Regularly updating beneficiary designations, especially after significant life events, is essential to prevent unintended consequences.
- For minor children, consider trusts or custodial accounts to manage assets until adulthood and select a guardian for their care.
- When beneficiaries have special needs, use a Special Needs Trust (SNT) to provide for them without jeopardizing government benefits.
- To prevent beneficiary conflicts, communicate estate plans clearly, use no-contest clauses judiciously, and appoint an impartial executor.
- Charitable bequests can reduce estate taxes and support causes important to the benefactor, ensuring the charity is a qualified 501(c)(3) organization.
- Estate planning should reflect one's values and intentions, and consulting with an estate planning attorney can help navigate the complexities involved.

3

WILLS AND TRUSTS

The Role of a Will in Estate Planning

Regarding estate planning, one of the most fundamental tools at your disposal is a will. In its simplest form, a will is a legal document that outlines your wishes regarding the distribution of your assets and the care of any minor children upon your death.

It is the cornerstone of a primary estate plan and serves as your voice to express your intentions when you are no longer here.

The role of a will in estate planning cannot be overstated. It provides instructions for managing and distributing your estate, including everything you own—your home, car, bank accounts, personal possessions, and more. Without a will, these decisions fall to state laws, which may not align with your wishes or the needs of your beneficiaries.

One of the primary benefits of having a will is the ability to choose an executor. You designate This person to carry out the instructions in your will, manage your estate, settle debts, and distribute your assets as directed. Choosing a trusted individual as your executor ensures your estate is handled according to your preferences.

Additionally, for those with minor children, a will is the vehicle through which you can appoint a guardian. This is one of the most critical decisions you can make, as it determines who will be responsible for raising your children if you cannot do so. Without a will, the court will decide who will take on this role, which may not coincide with your wishes.

It's also important to understand that a will does not cover certain assets. These include life insurance policies, retirement accounts, and assets held in joint tenancy or with designated beneficiaries. These pass outside the will directly to the named beneficiaries and are essential to your overall estate plan.

While a will is a powerful tool, it does have limitations. For instance, it does not provide any tax advantages. It cannot help your estate avoid probate—the legal process through which a will is validated, and your estate is settled. Probate can be time-consuming and costly, making your estate matter a public record matter.

For those seeking to manage their estate more privately or who wish to provide for their beneficiaries in a specific way, such as setting up conditional distributions or protecting assets from creditors, trusts can be an invaluable addition to a will. Trusts come in various forms and serve different purposes, which we will explore in detail in the following section. They can offer more control over your assets, potential tax benefits, and the ability to bypass the probate process, among other advantages.

In conclusion, a will is a critical element of any estate plan. It ensures that your wishes regarding the distribution of your assets and the care of your children are known and respected. However, it is just one part of a comprehensive estate plan, which may include tools like trusts to thoroughly address your needs and goals. Understanding a will's strengths and limitations helps you make informed decisions about protecting your legacy and providing for your loved ones.

Types of Trusts

As we delve into estate planning, we've already explored the significance of wills in ensuring your wishes are honored after you pass away. Now, let's shift our focus to trusts, another essential tool that can offer additional flexibility and control over managing and distributing your assets.

A trust is a fiduciary arrangement allowing a third party, or trustee, to hold assets on behalf of a beneficiary or beneficiary. Trusts can be arranged in many ways and specify how and when the assets pass to the beneficiaries. They come in various types, each with its own rules and purposes, and choosing the right one depends on your circumstances and goals.

- **Revocable Trusts**, also known as living trusts, are created during your lifetime and can be altered or revoked before death. They help avoid probate, the legal process of distributing your estate, which can be costly and time-consuming. With a revocable trust, you maintain control over the trust assets. You can act as the trustee, managing the property and assets held in the trust.

- **Irrevocable Trusts**, in contrast, cannot be modified or terminated without the beneficiary's permission after they are created. This type of trust can benefit estate tax considerations, as the assets placed into the trust are no longer considered part of your estate for tax purposes. It's a way to reduce your taxable estate, potentially shielding your beneficiaries from high taxes and providing asset protection from creditors.
- **Testamentary Trusts** are created as part of a will and only come into effect after your death. This type of trust allows you to set conditions for your assets' distribution. For example, you might stipulate that the assets should only be distributed once the beneficiary reaches a certain age or meets specific milestones, like college graduation.
- **Charitable Trusts** are set up to benefit a particular charity or the public. A charitable remainder trust, for instance, can provide an income stream to you or another beneficiary, with the remainder of the trust going to charity. Conversely, a charitable lead trust allows you to give a fixed amount to charity for several years, eventually passing the remaining assets to your beneficiaries.
- **Special Needs Trusts** are designed to benefit individuals with disabilities without disqualifying them from government assistance programs like Medicaid or Supplemental Security Income (SSI). These trusts can pay for expenses that enhance the beneficiary's quality of life while preserving their eligibility for public benefits.
- **Spendthrift Trusts** protect a beneficiary's inheritance from their potential creditors by prohibiting the

beneficiary from selling or giving away their interest in the trust. It can also protect the assets from beneficiaries who might need to be financially savvy or prone to overspending.

- **Life Insurance Trusts** are irrevocable trusts that own a life insurance policy on your life. The death benefit from the policy can provide liquidity to your estate, pay estate taxes, or provide for your beneficiaries without the proceeds being subject to estate tax.

Understanding the nuances of each type of trust can be complex, but the effort is worthwhile. Trusts can offer a range of benefits, including tax advantages, asset protection, and ensuring that your wishes are carried out with precision. As you consider your estate planning options, consider your specific needs, the needs of your beneficiaries, and how different trusts might serve those needs. Remember, the right trust can be a powerful component of a comprehensive estate plan, working in concert with your will to achieve your ultimate goals.

Choosing Between a Will and a Trust

Regarding estate planning, one of the most critical decisions you'll make is whether to establish a will, a trust, or both. Understanding the differences between these two legal instruments and the unique benefits each offers is essential to making an informed choice that aligns with your circumstances and goals.

A will, also known as a testament, is a legal document articulating your wishes regarding the distribution of your assets and the care of any minor children upon your death. It is relatively straightforward to create and can effectively ensure that your estate is handled according to your preferences. One of the primary advantages of a will is its simplicity; it allows you to state clearly who gets what, and it can be updated as your situation changes. However, a will goes through probate, a public and often lengthy legal process where a court oversees the distribution of your estate. This can sometimes be costly and time-consuming for your heirs.

On the other hand, a trust is a more complex legal entity that can provide greater control over how your assets are managed and distributed, both during your lifetime and after your death. Trusts come in various types, as discussed in the previous section, and they can offer several advantages over wills. For instance, a trust can help your estate avoid probate, potentially saving time and maintaining privacy. Trusts can also provide tax benefits and protect your assets from creditors and legal judgments. Moreover, they can be structured to support beneficiaries over time, such as children or relatives with special needs, rather than providing a single lump-sum inheritance.

Choosing between a will and a trust—or deciding to use both —depends on multiple factors, including the size and complexity of your estate, your privacy concerns, your financial goals, and the needs of your potential heirs. A will might suffice if you have a smaller estate and straightforward wishes. A trust could be more appropriate for larger estates or more complex situations, such as owning property in multiple states or wanting to provide for a beneficiary with special needs.

It's also worth noting that the two are not mutually exclusive. Many people opt for a 'pour-over' will in conjunction with a trust. This will simply state that assets not already included in the trust should be transferred upon your death.

Ultimately, the choice between a will and a trust is personal and should be made carefully considering your unique situation. It's highly recommended to consult with an estate planning attorney who can guide you through the nuances of each option and help you craft a plan that best meets your needs and ensures your legacy is preserved as you intend.

As you move forward in your estate planning journey, the next step after deciding between a will and a trust is to understand the process of creating a will, which we will explore in the following section. This will give you a solid foundation to begin drafting this crucial document, should you choose it as part of your estate plan.

The Process of Creating a Will

Having decided that a will is the appropriate tool for your estate planning needs, the next step is understanding the process of creating a will. This document, often considered the cornerstone of an estate plan, outlines your wishes regarding the distribution of your assets and the care of any minor children after your passing. Let's walk through the steps to create a will, ensuring that your final wishes are honored and your loved ones are provided for according to your desires.

Step 1: Inventory Your Assets. Begin by making a comprehensive list of your assets. This includes your real estate properties, bank accounts, investment accounts, retirement funds, insurance policies, and personal property of value, such as jewelry, art, and vehicles. Also, consider digital assets such as online accounts or digital currencies. Knowing what you own is critical to effectively distributing your estate.

Step 2: Decide on Beneficiaries. After you've listed your assets, decide who will inherit them. Beneficiaries can include family members, friends, charitable organizations, or institutions. Be clear about who gets what, as ambiguity can lead to disputes among your heirs. If you have minor children, consider appointing a guardian to care for them.

Step 3: Choose an Executor. An executor is the person who will carry out the instructions of your will. Choose someone responsible and trustworthy, as this person will manage your estate's affairs, from paying off debts to distributing assets to your beneficiaries. It's also wise to name an alternate executor in case your first choice is unable or unwilling to serve.

Step 4: Draft Your Will. While it's possible to draft a will on your own, especially with online templates, working with an attorney is often advisable. A legal professional can ensure that your will complies with state laws and that your wishes are articulated. They can also help you navigate complex situations, such as providing for a special needs family member or structuring inheritances to minimize taxes.

Step 5: Sign Your Will in the Presence of Witnesses. For a will to be legally valid, it must be signed by at least two witnesses. These witnesses must be adults who are not beneficiaries of the will and can attest to your mental capacity when signing. Some states may also require the will to be notarized.

Step 6: Store Your Will Safely. Once signed, your will should be stored in a safe location, such as a fireproof safe or a safety deposit box. Ensure that your executor knows where to find your will and how to access it when the time comes. It's also a good idea to keep a list of your assets and their locations with the will for easier estate management.

Step 7: Review and Update as Necessary. Life changes such as marriage, divorce, the birth of children, or the acquisition of significant assets necessitate an update to your will. Review your will periodically and after major life events to reflect your wishes. Any changes should be made with the same formalities as the original will, including the signing and witnessing process.

Creating a will is a proactive step in managing your estate and can bring peace of mind to you and your loved ones. It's fundamental to ensuring that your legacy is passed on as you envision it. With your will in place, you can consider how trusts further enhance your estate planning strategy, offering additional layers of management and protection for your assets.

How Trusts Can Manage and Protect Assets

In estate planning, trusts emerge as a versatile tool, offering many benefits beyond the primary distribution of assets after one's passing. Trusts can be particularly effective for managing and protecting assets, both during one's lifetime and after. Understanding how trusts function and the advantages they provide is crucial for anyone looking to establish a comprehensive estate plan.

One of the primary ways trusts can manage assets is through their ability to set terms for how and when assets are distributed. This level of control is particularly beneficial for those who wish to provide for their beneficiaries over time rather than in a single lump sum. For instance, a trust can be set up to disburse funds when a beneficiary reaches certain milestones, such as college graduation or age.

Trusts also offer a degree of asset protection. By placing assets within a trust, they are generally shielded from creditors and legal judgments against the beneficiaries. This is because the assets are no longer considered the beneficiaries' personal property but rather the trust's property. This protection can be invaluable for beneficiaries at higher risk of legal action, such as professionals in litigious fields or individuals with significant debt.

Another protective feature of trusts is their ability to preserve privacy. Unlike wills, which become public documents once they go through probate, trusts typically do not. This means the details of your assets and whom you have chosen to benefit from them can remain private, away from the prying eyes of those outside the intended circle of trust beneficiaries and trustees.

For families with special needs individuals, trusts can be particularly beneficial. A special needs trust can be established to ensure that a beneficiary who receives government benefits will not be disqualified from such assistance due to an inheritance.

The trust can provide supplemental resources without affecting the beneficiary's eligibility for public assistance programs.

Moreover, trusts can be used to manage and protect assets in the event of the trustor's incapacity. Through a living trust, you can appoint a trustee to manage your affairs without needing a court-appointed guardian or conservator should you become unable to manage your affairs. This can provide peace of mind, knowing that your assets are in trusted hands and that your wishes regarding their management will be respected.

In conclusion, trusts are a powerful component of estate planning that can offer significant advantages in managing and protecting assets. Whether your goal is to provide for your loved ones, protect your assets from creditors, or ensure privacy in the distribution of your estate, trusts can be tailored to meet those needs. As with any legal matter, it's wise to consult an estate planning attorney who can guide you through the intricacies of trust creation and help you determine the best type of trust for your circumstances.

Chapter Summary

- A will is a legal document that outlines asset distribution and care of minor children after death.
- State laws determine estate distribution without a will, which may not reflect personal wishes.
- Wills allow for the appointment of an executor and, for those with minor children, a guardian.
- A will does not cover certain assets like life insurance and retirement accounts.
- Wills do not offer tax benefits and do not avoid probate, which is public and can be costly.
- Trusts can be used alongside wills for more control, tax benefits, and bypass probate.

- Trusts come in various forms, such as revocable, irrevocable, testamentary, charitable, special needs, spendthrift, and life insurance trusts, each serving different purposes.
- Choosing between a will and a trust depends on individual circumstances, estate size, and complexity, with many opting for both to address different aspects of estate planning.

4

TAXES AND ESTATE PLANNING

Understanding Estate Taxes

When we talk about estate planning, one of the most critical aspects to understand is estate taxes. These are the taxes that your heirs may need to pay on the assets they inherit after you pass away. It's a common concern for many individuals who wish to leave as much as possible to their loved ones rather than to tax collectors.

Estate taxes, often called "death taxes," are levied by the federal government and, in some cases, state governments. The amount of tax due is calculated based on the estate's value at the time of the deceased's passing. It's important to note that not all estates are subject to estate taxes; there are exemption limits that change over time due to legislation and inflation adjustments.

As of the time of writing, the federal estate tax exemption is relatively high, meaning that only estates valued above a certain threshold are required to pay estate taxes. This exemption limit effectively removes the majority of estates from the federal estate tax's reach. However, the tax rate can be significant for those with assets exceeding this exemption amount, often rising to a substantial percentage of the estate's value.

It's also worth noting that some states have their own estate or inheritance taxes with different exemption levels and rates. Therefore, knowing the laws specific to your state is crucial when planning your estate.

One of the critical strategies in estate planning is to legally reduce the size of your taxable estate to minimize or avoid estate taxes. This can be done through various methods, such as making charitable donations, establishing trusts, or gifting assets during your lifetime. This leads us to gift taxes and their role in estate planning.

Gift taxes are closely related to estate taxes. They are a federal tax imposed on the transfer of property by gift during the giver's lifetime. The purpose of the gift tax is to prevent individuals from avoiding estate taxes by giving away their assets before they die. Just like estate taxes, there are annual and lifetime gift tax exemptions; understanding these can be a powerful tool in estate planning.

By making strategic gifts within these exemption limits, you can effectively transfer wealth to your beneficiaries. At the same time, you're still alive, reducing the value of your estate and potentially lowering the estate tax burden upon your death. However, it's essential to approach this carefully, as improper gifting can lead to unintended tax consequences.

In the next section, we'll delve deeper into how gift taxes work and how they can influence your estate planning strategy, ensuring you can make informed decisions that benefit you and your heirs.

Gift Taxes and How They Affect Estate Planning

As we delve into the intricacies of estate planning, it's crucial to understand not only the estate taxes discussed earlier but also the role of gift taxes and how they can influence your estate planning strategy. Gift taxes are a vital piece of the puzzle, and their implications can help you make more informed decisions about transferring wealth during your lifetime.

Gift taxes are federal taxes applied to transferring property or money to another person. At the same time, you are still alive without expecting to receive something of equal value in return. The key to gift taxes is a 'taxable gift.' Not all gifts are taxable, thanks to the annual gift tax exclusion. For instance, as of the time of writing, you can give up to $16,000 to any individual in a year without incurring a gift tax. If you're married, you and your spouse can each give $16,000, allowing for a combined gift of $32,000 to a single recipient without triggering the gift tax.

But what happens if you decide to be more generous and gift an amount that exceeds the annual exclusion? In that case, you'll need to file a gift tax return. However, filing a return doesn't necessarily mean you'll have to pay a tax. There's also a lifetime gift tax exemption that comes into play. This exemption is the total amount you can give away throughout your lifetime, above and beyond the annual exclusions, without paying gift taxes. The lifetime exemption amount is linked to the estate tax exemption, as they are part of the same tax system.

It's important to note that the gift and estate tax exemptions are unified. This means that the gifts you give during your lifetime that exceed the annual exclusion will reduce the amount you can leave tax-free at your death. For example, if you have a lifetime exemption of $11.7 million and make taxable gifts totaling $1 million during your lifetime, your remaining exemption that can be applied to your estate would be $10.7 million.

Understanding gift taxes is not just about knowing the numbers; it's about recognizing the opportunities and implications for your estate planning. For instance, making gifts within the annual exclusion limit can be a strategic way to reduce the size of your estate, potentially lowering estate taxes upon your death. Additionally, paying for someone's tuition or medical expenses directly to the institution can be exempt from gift taxes, which can be another effective way to pass on wealth without incurring taxes.

As you consider how to manage your estate, remember that the rules surrounding gift taxes can change due to legislation, so it's wise to stay informed or consult a professional. In the next part of our discussion, we'll explore various strategies that can help you minimize taxes and maximize the financial legacy you leave behind. By proactively managing gift taxes and understanding their relationship with estate taxes, you can craft a more effective and efficient estate plan that reflects your wishes and benefits your loved ones.

Strategies to Minimize Taxes

As we've seen, taxes can significantly impact your estate and the legacy you leave behind. Fortunately, there are several strategies you can employ to minimize the taxes levied on your estate. By understanding these tactics and incorporating them into your estate plan, you can ensure that more of your assets go to your loved ones rather than to tax collectors.

1. **Utilize the Annual Gift Tax Exclusion:** One of the simplest ways to reduce your estate tax liability is to give gifts during your lifetime. As per the current tax laws, you can give a certain amount per year to as many individuals as you like without incurring gift tax. This reduces the size of your estate and allows you to see your beneficiaries enjoy their inheritance.

2. **Pay for Medical and Educational Expenses:** Besides the annual gift exclusion, payments made directly to a medical institution for someone's medical care or to an educational institution for tuition are exempt from gift tax. This can be a strategic way to support loved ones while decreasing your estate's value.

3. **Set Up Trusts:** Trusts can be a powerful tool in estate planning. Certain types of trusts, like irrevocable life insurance trusts, can remove the value of life insurance from your estate. Others, such as charitable remainder trusts, can provide income to beneficiaries before the remainder goes to a charity, which may also provide tax benefits.

4. **Take Advantage of the Marital Deduction:** If you are married, you can leave unlimited assets to your spouse tax-free, provided your spouse is a U.S. citizen. This marital deduction can be a cornerstone in planning to reduce estate taxes. Still, it's also essential to consider the eventual tax implications for your spouse's estate.

5. **Charitable Giving:** Donating to charity is not only a way to support causes you care about, but it can also reduce your estate tax liability. Bequests to charity are deductible from the value of your estate and can significantly lower the estate tax bill.

6. **Consider Lifetime Transfers:** Making transfers during your lifetime can be more tax-efficient than transferring wealth at death. This is because any appreciation on the assets after the

transfer would occur outside of your estate, potentially leading to significant tax savings.

7. **Explore Business Succession Planning:** If you own a business, there are specific strategies, such as selling your interest to a family member at a reduced value or setting up a family-limited partnership, that can help minimize taxes while ensuring a smooth transition of your business.

8. **Keep Up with Tax Law Changes:** Tax laws are constantly evolving, and strategies that are effective today may be less beneficial tomorrow. Staying informed about changes in tax legislation or working with a tax professional can help you adapt your estate plan to take advantage of new laws and avoid pitfalls.

Remember, each of these strategies comes with its own set of rules and limitations. It's crucial to work with an estate planning attorney and a tax advisor who can help tailor these strategies to your specific situation. By being proactive and informed, you can craft an estate plan that reflects your wishes and maximizes the financial benefits for your heirs.

State Estate and Inheritance Taxes

As we delve into estate planning, it's crucial to understand the federal tax implications and the state-specific nuances that can affect your estate. While the previous discussion focused on general strategies to minimize taxes, here we will navigate the often-overlooked terrain of state estate and inheritance taxes, which can significantly impact the legacy you leave behind.

Firstly, it's important to distinguish between estate taxes and inheritance taxes. The state levies estate taxes on the estate transfer before distribution to the beneficiaries. In contrast, inheritance taxes are imposed on the estate recipients after the assets have been distributed. Not all states impose these taxes, and those have varying rates and exemption thresholds.

For those states that impose estate taxes, the exemption

amounts—below which no taxes are due—can vary widely. Some states align with the federal exemption amount, while others set their own, often much lower, thresholds. This means that even if your estate is not subject to federal estate taxes, it could still owe state estate taxes.

Inheritance taxes, on the other hand, are even less common. Still, they can surprise beneficiaries living in states that impose them. These taxes are usually based on the beneficiary's relationship to the decedent. Typically, spouses are exempt, and the rates may be lower for direct descendants. More distant relatives and non-relatives may find themselves facing higher tax rates.

Understanding the rules in your state is essential. Suppose you live in a state with estate or inheritance taxes or own property in such a state. In that case, it's wise to consult with a local estate planning attorney or tax advisor who can provide guidance tailored to your situation. They can help you explore strategies to minimize these state taxes, such as gifting during your lifetime or establishing trusts.

Moreover, if you're considering moving to another state, be aware that the estate and inheritance tax landscape should factor into your decision. A state with no estate or inheritance taxes might favor your estate planning goals more favorably.

Remember, estate planning is not a one-size-fits-all process. Each state's laws can significantly influence the effectiveness of your estate planning strategies. By staying informed and seeking professional advice, you can navigate these state-specific taxes and help ensure your estate is passed on according to your wishes with minimal tax burden on your heirs.

As we continue to explore the intricacies of estate planning, it's clear that life insurance can play a pivotal role in managing estate taxes. This versatile tool can provide liquidity to pay estate taxes and other expenses, ensuring your beneficiaries are not burdened with unexpected financial obligations. But before we delve into the strategic use of life insurance, it's essential to have a solid understanding of the state tax implications that might affect your estate.

The Role of Life Insurance in Estate Taxes

Life insurance is a powerful tool in estate planning, particularly when managing estate taxes. Its role is multifaceted, offering financial protection for your beneficiaries and strategic advantages for your estate's tax liabilities. Understanding how life insurance can be used to address estate taxes will help you make informed decisions as you structure your estate plan.

When you pass away, your estate may be subject to federal estate taxes if its value exceeds the exemption threshold the Internal Revenue Service (IRS) set. As of the time of writing, this threshold is in the millions of dollars, but it's essential to stay updated as tax laws and exemption limits can change. Suppose your estate is large enough to owe estate taxes. In that case, the proceeds from a life insurance policy can be a source of liquidity to pay these taxes without the need to sell off assets.

One of the key benefits of life insurance is that the death benefit paid out to beneficiaries is generally income tax-free. This means your loved ones can receive significant money without worrying about a tax bill on those funds. However, the value of the life insurance policy is included in your estate for estate tax purposes if you own the policy at the time of your death. This inclusion could push your estate over the exemption limit and result in a higher tax liability.

To avoid having the life insurance proceeds included in your estate, consider creating an irrevocable life insurance trust (ILIT). You relinquish control by transferring ownership of the life insurance policy to the ILIT. As a result, the proceeds are not considered part of your estate when you die. This means they won't be subject to estate taxes. The trust becomes the policy owner and beneficiary. Upon your death, the trust distributes the proceeds to your designated beneficiaries according to the terms you've set forth.

It's important to note that setting up an ILIT and transferring your life insurance policy into it must be done correctly to ensure that it achieves the desired tax benefits. There are specific rules and potential pitfalls to be aware of, such as the three-year rule, which states that if you die within three years of transferring the policy to the ILIT, the IRS will still consider the insurance proceeds as part of your estate. Therefore, planning and working with an experienced estate planning attorney is essential to navigate these complexities.

Additionally, life insurance can be used to provide for any potential liquidity needs your estate might have. For example, suppose your estate consists mainly of illiquid assets like real estate or a family business. In that case, your heirs might be challenged to obtain the cash needed to pay estate taxes. Life insurance proceeds can provide the necessary funds to cover these taxes without requiring your heirs to sell off assets, often at a hasty discount.

In summary, life insurance can play a pivotal role in estate planning by providing tax-free funds to beneficiaries, offering a means to pay estate taxes, and ensuring that your estate's assets are not unnecessarily liquidated to meet tax obligations. By considering the use of life insurance and an ILIT, you can create a more efficient and tax-effective estate plan. As with all aspects of estate planning, it's wise to consult professionals who can guide you through the process and help tailor a strategy to your specific needs and goals.

Chapter Summary

- Estate taxes or "death taxes" are levied on assets inherited after someone passes away, but only if the estate exceeds a specific exemption limit.
- The federal estate tax exemption is high, removing most estates from its reach. Still, the tax rate for eligible estates can be substantial.
- Some states have their own estate or inheritance taxes with different exemption levels and rates, which must be considered in estate planning.
- Gift taxes are imposed on property transferred during the giver's lifetime, with annual and lifetime exemptions to prevent avoidance of estate taxes.
- Strategic gifting within exemption limits can reduce the taxable estate size and lower the estate tax burden upon death.
- Utilizing the annual gift tax exclusion, paying for medical and educational expenses, setting up trusts, and charitable giving are strategies to minimize estate taxes.
- State estate and inheritance taxes vary, with different exemption amounts and rates, and should be factored into estate planning.
- Life insurance can provide liquidity to pay estate taxes and protect beneficiaries. Still, if owned by the deceased, it may increase estate tax liability unless placed in an irrevocable life insurance trust (ILIT).

5

HEALTHCARE DECISIONS AND ADVANCE DIRECTIVES

Healthcare Power of Attorney

Regarding estate planning, one of the most personal and significant decisions you can make is who will make healthcare decisions for you if you cannot do so yourself. This is where a Healthcare Power of Attorney (HPOA) becomes an essential part of your planning toolkit.

A Healthcare Power of Attorney is a legal document allowing you to appoint someone you trust, often called your agent or proxy, to make medical decisions on your behalf. If you are incapacitated, this person will have the authority to speak with your doctors, access your medical records, and make decisions about treatments, including life-sustaining measures.

Choosing your agent is a decision that should not be taken lightly. Someone who knows you well, understands your wishes, and is willing to advocate. It's also wise to select an alternate agent in case your primary choice is unable or unwilling to serve when the time comes.

When drafting a Healthcare Power of Attorney, being as transparent as possible about your preferences for medical care is essential. While it's impossible to anticipate every medical scenario, you can guide your general values and desires regarding quality of life, pain management, and any specific treatments you would or would not want.

One common misconception is that a Healthcare Power of Attorney is only for the elderly or those with chronic illnesses. However, unexpected medical situations can arise at any age, making it a prudent choice for any adult to have an HPOA in place.

After completing your Healthcare Power of Attorney, you must inform your chosen agent and discuss your wishes with them. You should also provide them with a copy of the document and inform your primary care physician and any specialists you see regularly. Keeping the document accessible, and perhaps even in an electronic format that can be easily shared, ensures that it can be quickly referenced when needed.

Remember, a Healthcare Power of Attorney can be revoked or changed if you are still competent. Life changes, such as marriage, divorce, or the death of your chosen agent, may necessitate a review and update of your HPOA. Regularly reviewing your estate planning documents ensures they reflect your current wishes and circumstances.

A Healthcare Power of Attorney is about maintaining control over your healthcare decisions, even when you cannot articulate them yourself. It's a powerful tool that provides peace of mind, knowing that your health and well-being will be in trusted hands if you cannot decide independently.

Living Wills and Medical Directives

In the realm of estate planning, preparing for the unexpected is a prudent step. While we've discussed the importance of designating someone to make healthcare decisions on your behalf through a healthcare power of attorney, it's equally crucial to delve into the specifics of your healthcare preferences. This is where living wills and medical directives come into play.

A living will is a written document that details your wishes regarding medical treatment in situations where you cannot communicate your decisions due to illness or incapacity. It's a proactive measure that provides clear instructions on what medical actions should be taken on your behalf. This can include your preferences on life-sustaining measures such as artificial hydration and nutrition, mechanical ventilation, or other forms of life support.

Creating a living will requires careful reflection on your values and beliefs about quality of life and end-of-life care. Discussing your wishes with family members and your healthcare provider is advisable to ensure they understand your preferences. Remember, living will become effective only under the specific conditions outlined in the document, typically when you are terminally ill or permanently unconscious with no expectation of recovery.

Medical directives, often used interchangeably with living

wills, can also encompass other types of instructions, such as organ donation preferences and pain management. These directives provide a comprehensive guide to healthcare professionals and loved ones, ensuring that your healthcare treatment aligns with your wishes.

It's important to note that living wills and medical directives are legally binding documents, and their validity can vary from state to state. Therefore, ensuring that your documents comply with your state's laws is essential. Also, have them reviewed by an attorney specializing in estate planning to confirm that they accurately express your intentions.

Once you have prepared your living will and medical directives, it's crucial to keep them accessible. Inform your healthcare power of attorney, family members, and primary care physician of their existence and location. Some individuals carry a card in their wallet indicating the presence of a living will and where it can be found.

In summary, living wills and medical directives are critical components of a comprehensive estate plan. They provide peace of mind, knowing that your healthcare wishes will be respected even when you cannot voice them. By taking the time to create these documents, you are not only making decisions for yourself but also easing the burden on your loved ones during challenging times.

As we continue to navigate the intricacies of healthcare decisions within estate planning, we must consider all scenarios, including the potential need for a Do Not Resuscitate order, which we will explore in the following discussion.

Do Not Resuscitate Orders (DNR)

As we delve further into healthcare decisions within estate planning, it's essential to understand the role of do-not-resuscitate orders, commonly known as DNRs. These specific medical orders can be a critical component of your advance directives. While living wills and medical directives outline a range of preferences for care, a DNR is a more focused document that addresses a particular situation: whether or not you wish to receive cardiopulmonary resuscitation (CPR) if your heart stops beating or you stop breathing.

A DNR is not a decision to be taken lightly, as it can determine the course of action medical personnel will take in a life-threatening situation. It's essential to consider your values, beliefs, and what quality of life means to you when deciding whether to have a DNR in place. This decision should be made after careful discussion with your healthcare provider, understanding such an order's potential outcomes and implications.

If you choose to have a DNR, it's crucial to ensure that this order is readily accessible to healthcare providers. Unlike other estate planning documents that might be stored away, a DNR must be immediately available in an emergency. This might mean having a copy at home, in your wallet, or registered with a hospital or primary care physician. Some states even have registries for such orders to ensure emergency responders can access them quickly.

It's also worth noting that DNR orders are not one-size-fits-all. They can be tailored to your specific health situation and preferences. For example, some people may want a DNR in place only if they have a terminal illness. In contrast, others may want it to apply regardless of their health status. The nuances of your DNR can be discussed with your healthcare provider to ensure that it aligns with your wishes.

Remember, a DNR is a legally binding document that will guide medical professionals in an emergency. Therefore, reviewing and updating it as your health status or preferences change is imperative. Like all aspects of estate planning, your decisions should reflect your current circumstances and wishes.

A DNR is a significant piece of your healthcare directive puzzle. It's a declaration of your wishes regarding life-saving measures and requires thoughtful consideration. As you plan for the future, remember that these healthcare decisions are as much a part of your legacy as your financial or material assets. They speak to the care you wish to receive and the dignity with which you choose to face life's most challenging moments.

The Importance of Communicating Your Wishes

In the estate planning journey, one of the most compassionate steps you can take is to ensure that your healthcare wishes are communicated to your loved ones and healthcare providers. This is not just about having the documents in place but also about having the conversations that clarify your intentions.

Imagine a scenario where you cannot speak for yourself due to a medical condition. With clear instructions from you, your family may be able to guess what you want regarding medical treatment. This can lead to confusion, family disputes, and decisions that may align differently with your desires. To prevent this, it's essential to articulate your healthcare preferences through advance directives and communicate these wishes to those involved in your care.

Advance directives are legal documents that allow you to spell out your decisions about end-of-life care beforehand. They provide a way to communicate your wishes to family, friends, and healthcare professionals and to avoid confusion later on. These directives come in several forms, including living wills and durable powers of attorney for healthcare.

A living will is a written, legal document that spells out the types of medical treatments and life-sustaining measures you do and do not want. This could include your wishes regarding the use of dialysis, ventilation, resuscitation, tube feeding, and organ or tissue donation. On the other hand, a durable power of attorney for healthcare allows you to appoint someone you trust to make health decisions on your behalf if you cannot do so.

More than filling out these forms and tucking them away in a safe deposit box is required. It would help if you discussed your wishes in detail with the person or people designated to make decisions on your behalf. This can include family members, close friends, or a healthcare proxy. These conversations can be difficult, but they are crucial. They provide an opportunity to explain the values and experiences that have shaped your healthcare preferences. Moreover, they give your loved ones the clarity and confidence to make decisions that honor your wishes.

In addition to family and friends, your healthcare providers should also be informed of your advance directives. Ensure that copies of these documents are included in your medical records and that your primary care physician knows your preferences. This ensures that your wishes are known in an emergency and can be followed.

Remember, your healthcare wishes may evolve, so it's essential to review and update your advance directives periodically. Life changes such as a new diagnosis, the loss of a loved one, or changes in your personal beliefs can all influence your healthcare decisions.

Communicating your healthcare wishes is a continuous process, not a one-time event. It's about guiding those difficult decisions that may need to be made when you cannot make them yourself. By taking these steps, you can alleviate the burden on your loved ones and ensure that your healthcare preferences are respected, no matter what the future holds.

HIPAA Authorizations

In estate planning, understanding the role of HIPAA authorizations within the context of healthcare decisions is a critical component. HIPAA, which stands for the Health Insurance Portability and Accountability Act, is a federal law that, among other things, protects the privacy of an individual's health information. When planning for the future, it's important to consider who will have access to your medical records if you cannot communicate your wishes directly.

A HIPAA authorization is a legal document allowing individuals to receive information about their health status. This is separate from a healthcare power of attorney or an advance directive. However, they often work in conjunction with one another. While a healthcare power of attorney designates someone to make healthcare decisions on your behalf, a HIPAA authorization provides that person, or any other individuals you choose, with the necessary access to your medical information to make informed decisions.

Creating an HIPAA authorization involves specifying the individuals you wish to grant access to your medical records. This could be a spouse, adult children, other family members, or close friends. Trusting that the individuals you name will respect your privacy while also advocating for your health care preferences is essential.

When drafting a HIPAA authorization, you can define the scope of the information disclosed. You could allow full access to your medical records or limit it to certain types of information. Additionally, you can set an expiration date for the authorization or state that it remains in effect until you revoke it.

It's also worth noting that even your closest family members may be denied access to your medical information without HIPAA authorization. This can be particularly distressing in emergencies when timely knowledge of your medical history, allergies, or medications could influence the care you receive.

To ensure that your HIPAA authorization effectively serves its purpose, it's advisable to consult with an attorney who specializes in estate planning. They can help you navigate the complexities of the law and tailor the document to your specific needs. Once completed, copies of your HIPAA authorization should be given to your healthcare providers, the individuals you've authorized, and possibly your attorney.

Remember, a HIPAA authorization is a safeguard, ensuring that those you trust can access the information necessary to advocate for your care according to your wishes. It's a vital piece of the healthcare puzzle in estate planning, complementing other advance directives and ensuring a comprehensive approach to your future healthcare decisions.

Chapter Summary

- A Healthcare Power of Attorney (HPOA) allows you to appoint someone to make medical decisions if you're incapacitated.
- Choosing a trusted individual as your agent and clearly outlining your medical care preferences in the HPOA is essential.
- Living wills and medical directives specify your wishes for medical treatment and end-of-life care, including life-sustaining measures.
- Do Not Resuscitate Orders (DNRs) indicate whether you want CPR if your heart stops or you stop breathing.
- Clear communication of your healthcare wishes to loved ones and healthcare providers is crucial to prevent confusion and disputes.

- Advance directives, including living wills and durable powers of attorney for healthcare, should be discussed with those who may be involved in your care.
- HIPAA authorizations allow specified individuals to access your medical records to make informed decisions on your behalf.
- Regularly reviewing and updating all healthcare directives is essential to ensure they reflect your current wishes and circumstances.

6

PROTECTING YOUR ESTATE

Asset Protection Strategies

As we delve into asset protection strategies within estate planning, it's crucial to understand insurance's role in safeguarding your financial legacy. Insurance acts as a buffer against unforeseen events that could erode your estate's value or burden your heirs with unexpected liabilities.

One of the primary insurance measures that can be employed is life insurance. A well-structured life insurance policy can provide immediate liquidity to your estate upon passing. This infusion of cash can be instrumental in covering estate taxes, debts, and other obligations without requiring your heirs to hastily liquidate assets, which might otherwise be sold at an inopportune time or a loss. Moreover, life insurance proceeds are generally income tax-free to beneficiaries, which makes them an efficient tool for transferring wealth.

Another vital insurance strategy involves the use of disability insurance. While often overlooked, disability insurance is a cornerstone of a comprehensive estate plan. If you cannot work due to illness or injury, disability insurance can replace a portion of your income. This ensures that your financial needs are met without dipping into the savings and investments earmarked for your estate, thereby preserving the value you intend to pass on to your heirs.

Long-term care insurance is also a critical component of protecting your assets. The cost of long-term care, whether in-home care or a stay in a nursing facility, can be staggering and quickly deplete an estate. By securing long-term care insurance, you can shield your assets from these significant expenses, ensuring that your estate remains intact for your beneficiaries.

In addition to life, disability, and long-term care insurance, property and casualty insurance should not be neglected. This type of insurance protects against losses to your tangible assets, such as your home, automobiles, and personal property. Adequate coverage can prevent scenarios where your estate becomes liable for damages exceeding your policy limits, which could result in the need to liquidate assets to cover these costs.

Lastly, consider an umbrella liability policy. This form of insurance provides an extra layer of protection above and beyond the limits of your homeowners and auto insurance policies. In the event of a lawsuit, an umbrella policy can help protect your estate from being eroded by legal judgments or settlements that exceed standard policy limits.

Incorporating these insurance strategies into your estate plan is more than a one-size-fits-all proposition. It requires careful evaluation of your unique circumstances, including your assets, family structure, and long-term objectives. Consulting with insurance professionals and estate planning attorneys can help tailor these protective measures to fit your needs, ensuring your estate is well-defended against life's unexpected twists and turns.

By thoughtfully integrating insurance into your estate planning, you create a robust shield around the wealth you've worked so hard to accumulate. This provides peace of mind but also secures the financial well-being of your loved ones for the future.

Insurance as a Protective Measure

In the realm of estate planning, one of the most effective tools for safeguarding your financial legacy is insurance. While insurance is widely understood in the context of health or auto protection, its role in estate planning should be more appreciated. Yet, it is a critical component in a comprehensive plan to protect your assets and fulfill your wishes after passing.

Insurance can serve as a protective measure in several ways. Firstly, life insurance is a cornerstone of estate planning. It provides a death benefit to your beneficiaries, which can help cover living expenses, pay off debts, and maintain their standard of living when you are no longer there to provide for them. It can also be used to pay estate taxes, thus preserving the estate's value for your heirs. The key is to ensure that the amount of coverage is adequate to meet the needs of your beneficiaries and aligns with your overall estate plan.

Another aspect of insurance that is essential for estate protection is disability insurance. This coverage replaces income if you cannot work due to a disability. It ensures that you and your family can meet financial obligations and maintain your lifestyle without depleting your savings or investments, which are likely a part of your estate.

Long-term care insurance is another protective measure that can preserve your estate. The cost of long-term care, whether in-home care or a stay in a nursing facility, can be excessive and quickly erode your savings. With long-term care insurance, you can cover these costs without liquidating assets you intend to pass on to your heirs.

Annuities can also play a role in protecting your estate. Certain annuities can provide a steady stream of income for life, which can be particularly useful if you outlive your other retirement savings. They can also offer death benefits to your beneficiaries.

It's important to note that your insurance policies' ownership and beneficiary designations should be carefully considered as part of your estate plan. Incorrect designations can lead to unintended consequences, such as benefits being subject to probate or going to unintended recipients. Therefore, it's crucial to review these designations regularly and update them as necessary, especially after significant life events like marriage, divorce, or the birth of a child.

In summary, insurance is not just about managing risks during your lifetime; it's also about ensuring that your estate is protected and can provide for your loved ones according to your wishes after you're gone. By integrating insurance into your estate plan, you can create a safety net that preserves your legacy and provides peace of mind.

The Role of Liability Coverage

When it comes to safeguarding your estate, understanding the role of liability coverage is crucial. Liability coverage serves as a shield, protecting your assets from potential claims that could arise from various incidents. This type of insurance is not just about covering the costs of a lawsuit; it's about preserving the legacy you've worked so hard to build for your beneficiaries.

Imagine for a moment that you're found responsible for an accident that causes significant injury to another person. The legal and medical expenses could be substantial. Without adequate liability coverage, your estate could be at risk to cover these costs. This is where liability insurance steps in, providing a financial buffer that can help protect your estate's value.

There are different types of liability coverage to consider. Homeowner's insurance, for example, typically includes a certain amount of liability protection in case someone is injured on your property. Auto insurance policies also include liability coverage for accidents while operating your vehicle. However, these standard policies often have coverage limits that may need to be revised to protect your assets fully in case of a severe claim.

This is where umbrella insurance policies become particularly valuable. An umbrella policy provides additional liability coverage beyond the limits of your other policies. It kicks in when the liability on these other policies has been exhausted, offering an extra layer of security. This policy is a critical component of estate protection for individuals with significant assets, as it extends coverage to one asset and potentially all of your assets.

Moreover, liability coverage can also protect against the unforeseen and the unpredictable. For instance, if you volunteer on the board of a local non-profit and a lawsuit is brought against the organization, your assets could be at risk if you don't have the appropriate liability coverage.

When evaluating your need for liability coverage, consider the total value of your assets, including your home, investments, and any businesses you own. The more you have at stake, the more coverage you should consider to ensure your estate is not depleted by a single claim or lawsuit. It's also wise to review your coverage periodically, especially after significant life events like purchasing a new home, starting a business, or acquiring valuable assets.

In essence, liability coverage is not just about protecting your wealth today; it's about ensuring that your estate plan stands firm against potential threats tomorrow. By incorporating sufficient liability coverage into your estate plan, you're taking a proactive step to shield your assets and secure the financial future of your loved ones.

Homestead Protections

As we delve into homestead protections within estate planning, it's essential to understand that your home is not just a physical shelter but also a cornerstone of your financial security. Homestead protections are legal provisions designed to safeguard a person's home's value from certain creditors during financial distress or upon the homeowner's death.

At its core, a homestead exemption allows you to declare a portion of your home's value as exempt from certain types of creditors' claims. This means that, up to a specific value, your home cannot be forced into sale by the claims of unsecured creditors. However, it's important to note that this protection does not extend to secured creditors, such as mortgage lenders or those holding liens against the property.

The extent of homestead protections can vary significantly from one state to another. Some states offer generous exemptions that protect a large portion of the home's value if not all. Other states may provide more modest protections, and a few may have restrictions that make the exemptions applicable only to specific groups, such as older people or people with a disability.

You must typically file a declaration with the local county recorder's office to claim a homestead exemption. This declaration should state that the property in question is your primary residence and, thus, should be treated as a homestead. It's crucial to understand your state's specific process and requirements, as failing to properly declare your homestead can result in missing out on these valuable protections.

One of the critical benefits of homestead protections is that they can provide a sense of security for your family. In the event of your passing, the homestead exemption can help ensure that your loved ones have a place to live, as the exempted value of the home is often protected from claims against the estate.

Moreover, homestead protections can be particularly beneficial for those facing financial hardship. In the face of mounting debts, the knowledge that your home may be shielded from certain creditors can provide much-needed peace of mind and stability.

However, it's also essential to recognize the limitations of homestead exemptions. They do not protect against all types of debts. For example, they typically do not protect against tax liens, alimony, or child support obligations. Additionally, creditors could target excess equity if you have equity in your home that exceeds the exemption limit.

In summary, homestead protections are a critical component of estate planning that can offer significant benefits. They provide a layer of security for your most valuable asset—your home—ensuring that it remains a sanctuary for you and your family, even in uncertain times. To fully leverage these protections, it's essential to understand the specific laws in your state and to take the necessary steps to claim your homestead exemption. Consulting with a knowledgeable estate planning attorney can help you navigate these waters and make the most of the protections available.

Protecting Assets from Creditors

In estate planning, safeguarding your assets from creditors is critical to ensure that your hard-earned wealth is passed on to your loved ones rather than being depleted by legal claims. While homestead protections can offer a shield for your primary residence, there are additional strategies to consider for the broader scope of your estate.

One such strategy is the use of trust. Trusts can be a powerful tool in estate planning, serving multiple purposes, including creditor protection. By placing assets into a trust, you effectively remove ownership from your estate and place it under the control of a trustee. This separation can protect those assets from creditors, as the assets are no longer yours but a trust property. There are various types of trusts, such as irrevocable trusts, which, once established, cannot be altered or revoked by the grantor. This irrevocability is critical to the trust's ability to protect assets from creditors.

Another method to consider is the establishment of retirement accounts, like IRAs and 401(k)s, which often come with statutory protections. These accounts are typically legally recognized as exempt from creditors' claims up to certain limits. It's essential to understand the specific protections offered by your state, as they can vary significantly.

Life insurance policies and annuities can also play a role in protecting your assets. The cash value of life insurance policies and the payouts from annuities are often protected from creditors, depending on your state's laws. These financial products must be structured correctly to ensure they provide the intended protection, so it's advisable to consult a financial advisor or estate planning attorney to navigate these options.

Asset protection should be considered an integral part of your estate planning process. It's also worth noting that timing is crucial; asset protection strategies are most effective when implemented before any claims or liabilities arise. Once a claim is made or even anticipated, transferring assets to protect them from creditors could be considered a fraudulent conveyance.

Lastly, maintaining proper insurance coverage is a straightforward yet vital component of protecting your estate. Liability insurance, umbrella policies, and other forms of insurance can provide a first line of defense against claims, preserving your estate's assets for your intended beneficiaries.

Remember, the goal of asset protection is not to evade legitimate debts or responsibilities but to ensure that you have a plan in place that safeguards your estate for the future you envision for your family. As with all aspects of estate planning, it's wise to seek professional advice tailored to your specific situation to ensure that your asset protection strategy is effective and compliant with current laws and regulations.

Chapter Summary

- Insurance is a critical component of estate planning, providing a financial safety net for unforeseen events.
- Life insurance offers immediate liquidity for estate taxes and debts, and proceeds are typically tax-free to beneficiaries.
- Disability insurance replaces income in case of inability to work, preserving estate value for heirs.
- Long-term care insurance covers the high care costs without depleting estate assets.
- Property and casualty insurance protects tangible assets, and umbrella policies offer additional liability coverage.
- Insurance policies should be carefully aligned with estate plans, with correct ownership and beneficiary designations.

- Liability coverage, including umbrella policies, protects assets from legal claims and lawsuits.
- Homestead protections shield a primary residence from certain creditors, with varying levels of protection by the state.

7

THE ROLE OF EXECUTORS AND TRUSTEES

Duties of an Executor

When someone passes away, their estate must be settled. This involves managing and distributing their assets according to their will, if one exists, or according to state laws if they died intestate, meaning without a will. The person responsible for this task is known as the executor. If you're new to estate planning, understanding the duties of an executor is crucial, as they play a pivotal role in ensuring that your final wishes are carried out correctly.

The executor's role begins immediately after death. Their first duty is to locate and review the deceased's will to understand its instructions and wishes. This document outlines who will inherit the assets and may contain specific distribution directions.

Once the will is located, the executor must file it with the appropriate probate court. Probate is the legal process through which the deceased's assets are appropriately distributed. The executor is responsible for navigating this process, which includes proving the will's validity, if necessary.

After initiating probate, the executor must take inventory of the deceased's assets. This can be a complex task, especially if the deceased owned extensive property or had a variety of investments. The executor must be thorough, ensuring that all assets are accounted for, from real estate and vehicles to stocks, bonds, and personal belongings.

The executor is also responsible for managing the deceased's financial responsibilities. This includes paying any outstanding debts and taxes. They must ensure that the estate's bills, such as utilities, mortgages, and credit card debts, are paid from its funds. Additionally, they must file final income tax returns on behalf of the deceased.

Another critical duty of the executor is to maintain the property until it can be distributed or sold. This may involve securing a vacant home, managing investment accounts, or ensuring that a business continues to operate smoothly.

Once debts and taxes are settled, the executor can distribute the remaining assets to the beneficiaries as outlined in the will. This process must be done with care to ensure that each beneficiary receives what they are entitled to. Suppose there are any disputes among the beneficiaries. In that case, the executor must handle these diplomatically and by the will and the law.

Finally, the executor must provide an accounting of all transactions they've made on behalf of the estate. This includes all expenses paid, debts settled, and distributions to beneficiaries. This accounting is typically presented to the probate court and the beneficiaries.

Being an executor is a significant responsibility that requires organization, attention to detail, and a fair amount of time. It's a role that should not be taken lightly, as the executor is entrusted with ensuring that the deceased's wishes are honored and their beneficiaries are cared for. As we move forward, we'll discuss how to select someone capable and willing to take on this vital role.

Selecting an Executor

In the estate planning journey, one of the pivotal decisions you'll make is selecting an executor for your will. This individual will manage your estate after you pass away, ensuring that your wishes are honored and your assets are distributed according to your instructions. Given the role's gravity, approaching this choice carefully is essential.

When considering whom to appoint as your executor, you should look for someone trustworthy but also organized, communicative, and capable of handling financial matters. It's not just about choosing someone close to you; it's about selecting someone who can navigate estate administration's complexities.

Start by considering the scope of your estate and the complexity of the tasks at hand. If your estate is relatively straightforward, a family member or a close friend who is diligent and detail-oriented might be a suitable choice. However, consider someone with legal or financial expertise or a professional executor for more complex estates, such as a trust company.

It's also essential to think about the potential burden on the executor. Administering an estate can be time-consuming and emotionally taxing, especially if it involves selling property, managing investments, or dealing with family disputes. Ensure the person you choose is willing and able to take on these responsibilities.

Another critical factor is the location of your executor. Ideally, they should be near most of your assets to facilitate easier management and reduce travel time and expenses. However, with today's technology, distance can be less of a barrier, provided the executor is comfortable with digital communication and document handling.

Before finalizing your decision, have a candid conversation with your potential executor. Discuss your expectations, the extent of the duties, and whether they feel comfortable taking on the role. Transparency at this stage can prevent misunderstandings and ensure that your estate is in good hands.

Lastly, it's wise to name an alternate executor in your will. Life is unpredictable, and if your primary choice cannot serve due to unforeseen circumstances, having a backup ensures that your estate will still be managed as you intended.

Remember, the role of an executor is significant, and the person you choose will have a lasting impact on how your legacy is carried out. Take your time, weigh your options, and choose someone who embodies the diligence and integrity required to honor your final wishes.

Duties of a Trustee

In estate planning, understanding the role of a trustee is as crucial as selecting one. A trustee is someone you appoint to manage the trust you've created, and their responsibilities are both broad and specific, governed by the terms of the trust agreement and state law. Let's delve into what it means to be a trustee and the duties of this vital role.

Firstly, a trustee must adhere to the trust's terms. This is the trustee's legal and moral compass. The trust document is like a roadmap; the trustee is the navigator, ensuring the trust's assets are managed and distributed according to the grantor's wishes. This means reading and understanding the document thoroughly, seeking legal advice, and executing the terms faithfully.

A trustee is also responsible for managing the trust's assets. This involves a prudent investment strategy that balances growth with risk, always considering the beneficiaries' best interests. The trustee must avoid speculative investments and ensure the trust's assets are productive. If the trust holds real estate, the trustee must maintain the property, collect rent, and pay expenses. The trustee must monitor performance and adjust if it holds financial assets.

Another critical duty is to maintain clear, accurate, and detailed records. This includes all income and expenses related to the trust, investments, distributions, and other financial transactions. These records are vital for tax purposes and reporting to beneficiaries entitled to information about the trust's administration.

Speaking of beneficiaries, the trustee must communicate with them regularly, providing updates on the trust's assets and the trustee's actions. This fosters transparency and trust, and it also helps to prevent misunderstandings or disputes.

The trustee also must file taxes for the trust. Trusts are subject to their own tax rules, and the trustee must ensure that all federal and state tax returns are filed on time and that any taxes due are paid from the trust's assets.

Lastly, the trustee must be fair and impartial to all beneficiaries. This can be challenging, especially if the beneficiaries have conflicting interests or if the trustee has a personal relationship with them. The trustee must navigate these relationships carefully, always acting reasonably and in line with the trust's terms.

Being a trustee is a significant responsibility, requiring diligence, fairness, and a commitment to acting in the best interests of the beneficiaries. It's not a role to be taken lightly, and it's essential for anyone creating a trust to choose their trustee wisely. With the right person in place, trust can be a powerful tool for managing and protecting assets for the benefit of loved ones.

Selecting a Trustee

After understanding the responsibilities that come with the role of a trustee, as outlined in the previous section, you're now faced with the crucial decision of selecting the right individual or institution to manage your trust. This decision is not to be taken lightly, as the trustee will have significant control over your assets and the welfare of your beneficiaries after you're gone.

When choosing a trustee, consider the following attributes and qualifications to ensure that your estate is in good hands:

- **Trustworthiness:** Above all, the trustee must be someone you can trust implicitly. This person will manage your assets and make decisions that affect your beneficiaries' financial future. Look for someone with a solid moral compass who has demonstrated reliability and integrity in their personal and professional life.
- **Financial Acumen:** The trustee should understand financial matters, investments, and the legal responsibilities of trust management. Professionals can always be consulted and don't need to be a financial expert. Still, a solid grasp of financial concepts is essential.
- **Organizational Skills:** Managing trust requires much organization. The trustee must keep accurate records,

file taxes for the trust, and communicate effectively with beneficiaries. Someone who is detail-oriented and has strong administrative skills would be a good fit for this role.

- **Impartiality:** It's essential that the trustee can act impartially and in the best interest of all beneficiaries. This can be challenging if the trustee is also a beneficiary or has a close relationship with one. Sometimes, appointing an independent third party, such as a trust company or a professional trustee, can help ensure that decisions are made without bias.
- **Availability:** Serving as a trustee is not a one-time task; it's an ongoing responsibility that can last many years. Make sure the person you choose has the time and willingness to commit to managing the trust for as long as necessary.
- **Willingness to Serve:** Never assume someone is willing to take on the role of trustee. Have a candid conversation with your potential trustee to ensure they understand the duties involved and are willing to accept the responsibility.
- **Age and Health:** Consider the age and health of your potential trustee. Choosing someone likely to predecease you or become incapacitated could lead to complications. It's also wise to name a successor trustee who can step in if your first choice cannot fulfill their duties.

Sometimes, you may find that no individual in your circle meets all these criteria, or you may prefer to avoid burdening friends or family with the responsibility. In such instances, you can opt for a professional trustee like a bank or trust company. These entities have the expertise and resources to manage trusts effectively but charge fees for their services.

Remember, the trustee you select will be pivotal in carrying out your wishes and managing your legacy. Take your time, weigh your options, and choose someone who will honor your trust and act in the best interests of your beneficiaries. Once you have selected, the next step will be to ensure that your estate and trust administration is set up for smooth management, which we will explore further.

Managing Estate and Trust Administration

Having selected a trustee, it's essential to understand the practical side of what happens next. The administration of an estate or trust is a critical phase where the decisions of the executor or trustee come to life, impacting beneficiaries and the legacy of the deceased. As you embark on this journey, you'll find that managing an estate or trust is akin to steering a ship through a series of checkpoints, each with its rules and potential challenges.

Firstly, the executor or trustee must take inventory of the estate's assets. This includes everything from bank accounts, real estate, stocks, and bonds to personal items like jewelry and artwork. It's a meticulous process that requires attention to detail and, often, detective work. The goal is to establish a clear picture of what the estate comprises, which will be crucial for the next steps.

Once the inventory is complete, the executor or trustee secures these assets. This might involve changing locks on the property, updating account information, and ensuring that all assets are safe from theft or damage. It's a role that requires high responsibility and trustworthiness, as you're safeguarding someone's lifetime of hard work and investment.

The next task is to settle any debts and liabilities. Before beneficiaries receive their inheritance, the executor or trustee must pay all the deceased's outstanding debts. This might include final income taxes, personal loans, or credit card debts. It's essential to handle these obligations promptly and accurately to avoid any legal complications down the line.

After debts have been settled, the executor or trustee must manage the distribution of the estate according to the will or trust document. This is where your role becomes deeply personal, fulfilling the deceased's final wishes. It's a process that requires sensitivity and diplomacy, especially if multiple beneficiaries have different interests.

The executor or trustee must maintain clear and open communication with the beneficiaries throughout this process. They have a right to understand how the estate is being managed and when they can expect to receive their inheritance. Regular updates can help to build trust and reduce anxiety or conflict among the beneficiaries.

Finally, the executor or trustee must prepare and file all necessary tax returns for the estate. This can be a complex task, requiring a good understanding of tax laws and, often, the assistance of a professional accountant or tax advisor.

In summary, managing estate and trust administration is a multifaceted role that requires organizational skills, financial understanding, and a compassionate touch. It's about more than just numbers and legal documents; it's about honoring the wishes of someone who has placed their ultimate trust in you. As you navigate this process, remember that your role is both a privilege and a responsibility, and your actions will leave a lasting impact on the lives the estate touches.

Chapter Summary

- Executors are responsible for settling an estate, including managing and distributing assets according to the will or state laws if there is no will.

- Executors must locate the will, fill it with the probate court, inventory assets, manage financial responsibilities, and maintain the property until distribution.
- They must pay the deceased's debts and taxes, distribute assets to beneficiaries, handle disputes, and provide an accounting of all transactions.
- Selecting an executor requires considering trustworthiness, organizational skills, financial understanding, willingness to serve, and naming an alternate.
- Trustees manage trusts according to the trust document and state law, balancing growth with investment risk and maintaining clear records.
- Trustees must communicate with beneficiaries, file trust taxes, and act impartially and fairly to all beneficiaries.
- When selecting a trustee, consider trustworthiness, financial knowledge, organizational skills, impartiality, availability, willingness to serve, and age and health.
- Estate and trust administration involves inventorying assets, securing them, settling debts, distributing inheritance, communicating with beneficiaries, and filing tax returns.

8

PLANNING FOR INCAPACITY

Financial Power of Attorney

When considering the future and the unexpected twists it may hold, it's crucial to prepare not just for the distribution of your assets after you pass away but also for the possibility that you might one day be unable to manage your financial affairs due to incapacity. This is where a Financial Power of Attorney (POA) becomes essential in your estate planning toolkit.

A Financial Power of Attorney is a legal document that allows you to appoint someone you trust, often referred to as your "agent" or "attorney-in-fact," to manage your financial matters if you become incapacitated and unable to do so yourself. This person will have the authority to handle tasks such as paying your bills, managing your investments, and making other financial decisions on your behalf.

One of the primary benefits of having a Financial Power of Attorney in place is that it provides a clear directive and immediate authority to your chosen agent without needing court intervention. This can be exceptionally comforting, as it ensures that your financial matters will be handled according to your wishes by someone you have personally selected.

When drafting a Financial Power of Attorney, you have the flexibility to define the scope of your agent's powers. You can grant them broad authority to handle your financial affairs or limit their powers to specific tasks, accounts, or assets. Additionally, you can decide whether this power becomes effective immediately or only activates upon your incapacity, which a medical professional's evaluation can determine.

It's essential to choose an agent who is trustworthy and capable of managing financial matters prudently. This person should understand your values and wishes regarding your finances and be willing to act in your best interest. It's also wise to name a successor agent who can step in if your first choice is unable or unwilling to serve when the time comes.

Creating a Financial Power of Attorney requires careful consideration and, often, the guidance of a legal professional to ensure that the document is valid and reflects your intentions. Remember, the POA is revocable; you can change or cancel it anytime if you are mentally competent.

Without a Financial Power of Attorney, or if additional

support is needed, the court may appoint a conservator to oversee an incapacitated person's financial affairs. This process, known as conservatorship, can be lengthy, costly, and more restrictive, so having a POA is generally preferable for many individuals planning for potential incapacity.

The Role of Conservatorships

In the estate planning journey, we've explored the importance of designating a financial power of attorney—a trusted individual who can manage your financial affairs should you become unable to do so yourself. However, there may be circumstances where a power of attorney is not in place or a situation arises that falls outside the scope of this document. In such cases, the court may appoint a conservator to step in. Let's delve into the role of conservatorships and how they function as a safety net in estate planning.

A conservatorship is a legal relationship established by a court order, where a person or organization, known as the conservator, is appointed to manage the financial and personal affairs of an adult deemed incapable of doing so themselves due to physical or mental limitations. This legal arrangement is particularly relevant when an individual has not made prior arrangements for incapacity or when disputes arise regarding the designated power of attorney.

Establishing a conservatorship can be initiated by a family member, a close friend, or any interested party concerned about the individual's well-being. The court then evaluates the evidence, which often includes medical testimony, to determine whether the person in question, often referred to as the conservatee, cannot handle their affairs.

Once a conservator is appointed, they are granted the authority to make decisions on behalf of the conservatee. These decisions can range from handling financial transactions, managing investments, paying bills, and selling property to making choices about living arrangements, health care, and other personal matters if a separate conservator of the person is appointed.

It's important to note that conservatorships have a significant level of court oversight. Conservators must provide regular reports and account for their actions to ensure that they act in the conservatee's best interests. This oversight is designed to protect the conservatee from potential abuse or neglect.

While conservatorships can offer a vital safety net, they can also be restrictive. They may involve a loss of autonomy for the conservatee. For this reason, many individuals prefer to plan by creating durable powers of attorney and health care directives, which allow them to choose who will make decisions for them in the event of incapacity.

In the digital age, our lives are increasingly intertwined with technology, which brings us to another aspect of estate planning: managing your digital legacy. As we move forward, we'll explore how to ensure that your online presence is handled according to your wishes, just as carefully as your offline assets.

Managing Your Digital Legacy

In the digital age, our lives are increasingly intertwined with technology, creating a substantial online presence that can outlive us. This digital footprint, comprising emails, social media accounts, online banking, and even virtual assets like domain names or cryptocurrency, constitutes what is known as your digital legacy. As part of planning for incapacity, managing this aspect of your estate is crucial to ensure your digital life is handled according to your wishes should you become unable to do so yourself.

Firstly, take inventory of your digital assets. This includes listing all your online accounts, such as email, social media, financial, shopping, and any websites you own. For each, note down the login credentials and how you would like each account handled. Some platforms have protocols for deceased or incapacitated users, so it's worth investigating and incorporating them into your plan.

Next, consider appointing a digital executor. This is someone you trust to manage your digital assets in line with your instructions. This role can be part of a broader power of attorney, or you can designate a separate digital power of attorney specifically for your online content. Ensure this person is tech-savvy and understands the sensitivity and confidentiality required to handle your digital legacy.

It's also essential to understand the legal landscape. The Revised Uniform Fiduciary Access to Digital Assets Act (RUFADAA), adopted by most states, allows you to give legal authority to your designated representative to access your digital assets. However, this requires explicit consent through estate planning documents, so include such permissions in your will, trust, or power of attorney.

Lastly, provide clear instructions for managing or disposing of your digital assets. This might include deleting certain accounts, archiving digital photos, or transferring valuable assets to beneficiaries. Be as specific as possible to avoid ambiguity leading to disputes or confusion.

Remember, managing your digital legacy is an ongoing process. You must update your estate plan accordingly as you acquire new digital assets or as online services change their policies. By taking these steps, you can ensure that your digital life is as well-organized and respectfully handled as the rest of your estate when you can no longer manage it yourself.

Chapter Summary

- A Financial Power of Attorney (POA) allows you to appoint someone to manage your finances if you become incapacitated.
- The appointed agent can handle tasks like paying bills and managing investments with immediate authority without court intervention.
- You can define the scope of the agent's powers and decide when the POA becomes effective immediately or upon incapacity.
- It's essential to choose a trustworthy and financially savvy agent and to consider naming a successor agent.
- A POA is revocable and can be changed if you are mentally competent.
- Without a POA, a court may appoint a conservator to manage your affairs, which can be a lengthy and costly process.
- Conservatorships involve court oversight and can be restrictive. Still, they serve as a safety net when no POA exists.

9

ESTATE PLANNING FOR BUSINESS OWNERS

Assessing Your Business Assets

As a business owner, your company is likely one of your most significant assets, and its value can substantially impact your estate. Assessing your business assets is a critical step in estate planning and requires a thorough and strategic approach. Let's delve into how to effectively evaluate your business holdings to ensure they align with your long-term estate planning goals.

Firstly, you'll need to determine the fair market value of your business. This can be a complex process, often requiring the expertise of a professional business appraiser. They will consider various factors, including your company's financial history, market position, and future earning potential. It's essential to have an accurate valuation, as this will influence your estate planning decisions, such as how to distribute shares among heirs or whether to sell the business.

Next, take stock of your business's tangible and intangible assets. Tangible assets include physical items like property, equipment, and inventory, while intangible assets include patents, trademarks, and goodwill. Understanding the full scope of what your business owns is essential for creating a comprehensive estate plan.

It would help if you also considered your business's liabilities. Debts and other financial obligations must be addressed in your estate plan to ensure they don't burden your heirs. Knowing the extent of these liabilities will help you make informed decisions about life insurance, asset distribution, and other estate planning tools.

Moreover, if your business has multiple owners, you'll need to review any existing agreements that may affect the transfer of your interests. These agreements can dictate what happens to your share of the business upon your death, and they should be aligned with your personal estate planning objectives.

Lastly, it's crucial to keep your business assessment up-to-date. Regularly revisiting and revising your valuation and asset inventory will help you adapt to market and business changes, ensuring your estate plan remains relevant and practical.

By thoroughly assessing your business assets, you lay the groundwork for the next steps in your estate planning journey. This careful evaluation will clarify your plans and offer peace of mind, knowing that your business legacy is well-prepared for the transition to the next generation.

Buy-Sell Agreements

As a business owner, creating a buy-sell agreement is one of the most critical components of your estate planning. This legally binding document outlines what happens to your share of the business in case of your death, disability, retirement, or if you decide to leave the company. It's a contingency plan that protects not only your interests but also those of your business partners and your family.

A buy-sell agreement can be compared to a prenuptial agreement for your business. It sets the terms for a buyout, ensuring that the remaining business owners have the right or the obligation to buy the departing owner's share at a predetermined price and under specific conditions. This agreement is crucial because it provides a clear path for the business to continue and can prevent potential disputes among remaining owners or between owners and the departing owner's heirs.

There are several types of buy-sell agreements, and the one you choose will depend on the nature of your business and your specific needs:

- **Cross-Purchase Agreements:** This type is used when there are few co-owners. Each owner buys a life insurance policy for the other owners. In death, the surviving owners use the insurance proceeds to buy the deceased owner's share of the business.
- **Entity-Purchase Agreements:** Also known as a stock redemption plan, the company purchases the departing owner's share. The business will own each

owner's insurance policy and is responsible for the buyout.

- **Hybrid Agreements:** A combination of the two above allows the company and the individual co-owners to share the responsibility of buying out a departing owner's interest.

When drafting a buy-sell agreement, it's essential to consider how the buyout will be funded. Life and disability insurance are standard methods because they provide a funding source exactly when needed. However, the agreement might also include provisions for installment payments or other methods of financing the buyout.

Valuation of the business interest is another critical component of the buy-sell agreement. You'll need to decide how to determine the value of a business owner's interest. This could be a fixed price agreed upon by all owners, a formula based on the company's earnings or book value, or a process involving a professional business valuation during the buyout.

It's also essential to review and update your buy-sell agreement regularly. As your business grows and changes, the terms that made sense at one point may no longer be relevant or fair. Regular reviews, ideally with the assistance of a legal and financial advisor, ensure that the agreement continues to reflect the current state of the business and the wishes of all parties involved.

In conclusion, a well-structured buy-sell agreement is a cornerstone of business continuity planning. It provides a roadmap for the future of your business in the face of unforeseen events and helps ensure that your legacy endures. As you move forward with your estate planning, remember that the decisions you make today will shape the future of your business long after you're gone. With thoughtful planning and clear communication, you can create a lasting impact that benefits your family, business partners, and the enterprise you've worked hard to build.

Succession Planning

As a business owner, you've likely invested significant time, energy, and resources into building a successful enterprise. But what happens to your business when you can no longer lead it? This is where succession planning is an essential component of estate planning for business owners.

Succession planning is identifying and preparing new leaders to take over your business when you retire, become incapacitated, or pass away. It's about ensuring the continuity of your business and preserving the legacy you've worked so hard to create. With a clear succession plan, your business could avoid an uncertain future, which could affect not only your family's wealth but also the livelihood of your employees and the satisfaction of your customers.

To begin with, consider who is best suited to take over your business. This could be a family member, a trusted employee, or even an external candidate. Choosing someone with the right skills and vision is essential to keep the business thriving. Once you've identified potential successors, involve them early in the business, allowing them to gain the necessary experience and knowledge.

Next, you'll want to formalize the succession plan. This involves setting a timeline for the transition, defining the roles and responsibilities of the successor, and outlining the training process. It's also crucial to consider how ownership will be transferred. Will it be a gradual transfer of shares, a sale, or perhaps a gift as part of your estate?

Legal documentation is a crucial aspect of succession planning. Work with an attorney to draft a will, power of attorney, and other necessary legal documents supporting your succession plan. These documents will help ensure that your wishes are fulfilled and that the leadership transition happens smoothly.

Communication is another vital element of a successful succession plan. Communicating your plans to your family, your business's potential successor, and critical stakeholders is essential. Open and honest communication can prevent misunderstandings and conflicts that could jeopardize the future of your business.

Finally, review and update your succession plan regularly. As your business grows and changes, so too might your choice of successor or the transition structure. Regular reviews ensure that your plan remains relevant and practical.

In summary, succession planning is a proactive approach to safeguarding the future of your business. It's about making thoughtful decisions today to protect your business's value and ensure its success tomorrow. With a solid succession plan, you can rest assured that your business legacy will endure, providing peace of mind for you, your family, and all those connected to your enterprise.

Insurance for Business Owners

As a business owner, you've likely invested significant time, energy, and resources into building your enterprise. It's not just a source of income; it's a part of your legacy. That's why insurance plays a crucial role in estate planning for business owners. It serves as a safety net, ensuring that your business can continue to operate and support your loved ones even in your absence.

Let's start by discussing the types of insurance that are particularly important for business owners:

- **Life Insurance:** The cornerstone of any business owner's insurance strategy. A life insurance policy can provide the funds necessary to keep the business afloat during the transition period following your passing. The payout can help cover debts, pay for ongoing expenses, or fund a buy-sell agreement, which we'll touch on shortly.

- **Disability Insurance:** What if an illness or injury prevents you from running your business long before you pass away? Disability insurance can replace a portion of your lost income, helping maintain your living standard and keeping the business operational.
- **Key Person Insurance:** Your business may rely on one or a few individuals whose expertise and management are critical to its success. Key person insurance compensates the business if one of these vital individuals passes away or becomes incapacitated, providing the financial breathing room to find a replacement or restructure the company.
- **Buy-Sell Agreements Funded by Life Insurance:** A buy-sell agreement is a legally binding document that outlines what happens to a business when one of the owners dies or wishes to leave the company. Life insurance policies can be structured to fund these agreements, ensuring that there's capital available for the remaining owners to buy the departing owner's share without financial strain.
- **Property and Casualty Insurance:** While not directly related to your death or disability, property and casualty insurance protects the physical assets of your business from unforeseen events like fires, theft, or natural disasters. This type of insurance helps preserve your business's value for your heirs.
- **Liability Insurance:** This insurance protects your estate from claims that could arise from the operations of your business. Maintaining adequate coverage to

shield your assets and those of your estate from potential lawsuits is essential.

When selecting insurance policies, consider the following:

- **The Value of Your Business:** How much is your business worth, and how much insurance will be needed to cover its value? This is a complex calculation that often requires the assistance of a professional appraiser or accountant.
- **Your Succession Plan:** Your insurance must tie directly into your succession plan. Who will take over the business? Will it be sold? The answers to these questions will influence the type and amount of insurance you should carry.
- **The Structure of Your Business:** Are you a sole proprietor, or do you have partners? The structure of your business will affect the kind of insurance policies you'll need.
- **Your Personal and Business Debts:** Insurance can help ensure that any debts you've guaranteed won't burden your family or business.

In conclusion, insurance for business owners is not just about protecting your interests; it's about safeguarding the future of your business and the financial security of your family and employees. By carefully selecting the suitable types and amounts of insurance, you can create a robust estate plan that addresses the unique challenges of business ownership. Remember, the goal is to provide peace of mind for yourself and your loved ones, knowing that the business you've worked so hard to build is protected against life's uncertainties.

Transferring Ownership and Control

As a business owner, you've invested significant time, energy, and resources into building your enterprise. It's not just a business but part of your legacy. That's why transferring ownership and control is a critical component of estate planning for business owners. This process ensures your business thrives and supports your beneficiaries according to your wishes after you leave.

When considering the transfer of your business, starting with a clear succession plan is essential. This plan outlines who will take over the business: family members, a partner, key employees, or an outside buyer. It also details the conditions under which the transfer will occur, such as retirement, disability, or death.

One common strategy for transferring ownership is through a buy-sell agreement. This legally binding contract stipulates how a partner's share of the business may be reassigned if that partner dies or leaves the company. The agreement can be funded with life insurance policies to ensure sufficient funds are available to buy out the departing partner's interest, allowing for a smoother transition and financial stability for the business.

Another option is to gift the business to your heirs during your lifetime. This can be done gradually to minimize taxes and to allow you to maintain some control as your successors become more involved in business operations. Be mindful, however, of the gift tax implications and the annual exclusion limits.

For those wishing to keep the business in the family, a family limited partnership (FLP) or a family limited liability company (FLLC) can be helpful. These structures allow you to transfer business shares to family members over time, often at a reduced tax cost, while retaining control over the business's direction.

Suppose you're considering selling the business outright. In that case, it's crucial to have a professional valuation done to determine a fair market price. This valuation will be important not only for a potential sale but also for estate tax purposes. It's also wise to consult a financial advisor to understand how the sale will impact your retirement and estate planning goals.

Lastly, it's essential to consider the potential impact of estate taxes on your business. With proper planning, strategies such as trusts, charitable contributions, and other tax planning techniques can minimize the estate tax burden and ensure that your heirs are not forced to sell the business to cover tax liabilities.

Remember, transferring ownership and control of your business is not a one-size-fits-all process. It requires careful planning, consideration of all stakeholders, and, often, the guidance of legal and financial professionals. By taking the time to establish a comprehensive plan, you can help secure the future of your business and provide for your heirs in the manner you envision.

Chapter Summary

- Determine your business's fair market value with a professional appraiser's help.
- Inventory your business's tangible and intangible assets to create a comprehensive estate plan.
- Address business liabilities in your estate plan to prevent them from burdening your heirs.
- Review any existing agreements with co-owners that may affect the transfer of business interests.
- Keep your business assessment current to ensure your estate plan adapts to changes in the market and business.
- Establish a buy-sell agreement to dictate what happens to your share of the business upon death or departure.

- Succession planning is crucial for identifying and preparing new leaders to take over the business.
- Select appropriate types and amounts of insurance to protect the business and support your loved ones after you're gone.

10

KEEPING YOUR ESTATE PLAN CURRENT

When to Review Your Estate Plan

Creating an estate plan is akin to capturing a snapshot of your life at a particular moment. As time marches on, your life and your estate plan evolve. It's not a 'set it and forget it' affair. Regular reviews ensure your estate plan accurately reflects your current wishes and circumstances. But when exactly should you dust off your estate documents and give them a thorough look-over?

Firstly, it's wise to mark your calendar for a biennial review. Every two years, take the time to sit down with your estate planning documents and go through them with a fine-tooth comb. This regular check-up will help you catch any changes in tax laws, estate laws, or personal preferences since your last review.

However, life only sometimes adheres to a schedule, and certain events can necessitate an immediate review of your estate plan. Significant life changes are the most apparent triggers for a review. These can include a marriage or divorce, which alters your relationship status and significantly impacts your estate planning decisions and beneficiary designations. The birth or adoption of a child is another joyous occasion that should prompt you to update your estate plan to include provisions for your new family member.

Similarly, the death of a loved one, mainly if they were included in your estate plan as a beneficiary or executor, requires immediate attention to adjust your plan accordingly. A significant change in your financial situation, such as receiving a large inheritance, winning the lottery, or suffering a substantial financial loss, also warrants a fresh look at your estate plan to ensure it still serves your best interests.

Additionally, you've moved to a different state. In that case, it's crucial to review your estate plan to ensure it complies with the laws of your new home. State laws regarding estate taxes, probate, and other estate planning issues can vary widely, and what was valid in one state may not be in another.

Another reason to review your estate plan is a change in your health or that of a family member. Suppose you or a loved one has been diagnosed with a severe illness or disability. In that case, you may need to make adjustments to your estate plan to address long-term care needs, medical directives, or the management of your affairs should you become incapacitated.

Finally, if there have been changes in the laws that affect estate planning—such as tax law reforms—it's essential to understand how these changes might affect your estate and whether any adjustments are needed to optimize your plan.

Remember, keeping your estate plan current is not just about adjusting to the adverse or unforeseen events in life. It's also about capturing the positive changes and ensuring that your plan reflects your life's journey accurately. Regular reviews and updates after significant life events will help ensure that your estate plan reflects your wishes and provide peace of mind that your legacy will be handled as you intended.

Life Events that Affect Your Estate Plan

As we navigate through life's journey, our circumstances inevitably change. These shifts, both big and small, can significantly impact the relevance and effectiveness of your estate plan. Understanding which life events can trigger a need for updates is crucial for ensuring that your wishes are honored and your loved ones are protected. Let's explore some of these pivotal moments and how they intertwine with your estate planning efforts.

Firstly, marriage is a joyful event that significantly changes one's life. If you've recently tied the knot, it's essential to reflect this in your estate plan. Consider including your spouse in your will, designate them as beneficiaries on retirement accounts, or grant them powers of attorney. Conversely, divorce is a life event requiring a thorough review of your estate plan. Removing your former spouse from any roles they previously held in your will, trusts, or as a beneficiary is a step that should be considered.

The arrival of children or grandchildren is another momentous occasion that should prompt a review of your estate plan. You may need to appoint guardians for minor children, set up trusts to manage their inheritance or make provisions for their education and care. As children grow and their circumstances change, your estate plan should evolve to reflect these developments.

Significant changes in your financial situation also warrant a review of your estate plan. This could include receiving a large inheritance, experiencing a substantial increase or decrease in the value of your assets, or starting a business. These financial shifts can affect how you wish to distribute your assets and may introduce new considerations for tax planning.

Health is another critical factor that can influence your estate plan. A diagnosis of a severe illness or a disability might lead to adjustments in your healthcare directives or living will. It's essential to ensure that your wishes regarding medical treatment and end-of-life care are clearly documented and that the individuals you've designated to make decisions on your behalf are still the right choices.

Lastly, relocation to a different state or country can affect your estate plan due to varying laws and regulations. It's advisable to consult with an estate planning attorney in your new location to ensure your plan complies with local laws and continues to serve your interests.

Each life event is a call to action—a reminder to revisit and potentially revise your estate plan. By keeping your plan aligned with your current circumstances, you can rest assured that your intentions will be honored and your loved ones will be cared for according to your wishes. Remember, an estate plan is not a static document but a dynamic framework that should adapt as your life unfolds.

Updating Beneficiaries

As we navigate through the journey of life, our relationships and circumstances evolve, often in ways we couldn't have anticipated when we first drafted our estate plans. It's crucial to remember that your estate plan is a living document, one that should grow and change as you do. A key component of keeping your estate plan current is regularly updating your beneficiaries.

Beneficiaries are the individuals or entities you designate to receive your assets upon passing. These can include family members, friends, charitable organizations, or trusts. Your beneficiary designations are found in various documents, such as wills, life insurance policies, retirement accounts, and investment portfolios.

Why is updating beneficiaries so important? Life events such as marriages, divorces, births, and deaths can drastically alter your original intentions for your estate. For instance, if you've named your spouse as a primary beneficiary and later divorced, you may not want your ex-spouse to remain the recipient of your assets. Similarly, the joyous arrival of children or grandchildren might prompt you to include them in your estate plan.

To update your beneficiaries, you'll need to review all documents where they are named. Start with your will and trust, if you have one, and then move on to your life insurance policies and retirement accounts like IRAs and 401(k)s. For each account or policy, you'll typically need to request a change of beneficiary form from the financial institution or insurance company. Fill out these forms with the new beneficiary information and submit them according to the provider's instructions.

It's also wise to consider contingent beneficiaries who will inherit if your primary beneficiary cannot do so. This adds an extra layer of protection and ensures that your assets are distributed according to your wishes, even if unexpected circumstances arise.

Remember, beneficiary designations often supersede instructions in your will. This means that even if your will states something different, the assets in accounts with a named beneficiary will go directly to that beneficiary. Therefore, ensuring that all designations are consistent with your overall estate plan is imperative.

As you update your beneficiaries, it's also an excellent time to reflect on the overall distribution of your assets. Are you dividing your estate in a way that aligns with your values and goals? Are there charitable causes you'd like to support? These considerations can guide you in making thoughtful and meaningful updates to your beneficiary designations.

In conclusion, keeping your beneficiaries up-to-date is vital to maintaining an effective estate plan. It's a task that requires attention to detail and an understanding of how various life changes impact your ultimate wishes for your legacy. By regularly reviewing and revising your beneficiary designations, you can rest assured that your assets will be distributed according to your current intentions, providing peace of mind for you and your loved ones.

Revising Legal Documents

As you've taken the critical step of designating beneficiaries, which we've discussed earlier, it's equally crucial to ensure that all your legal documents within your estate plan are up-to-date. Life is ever-changing, and your estate plan should be a living document that reflects your current circumstances and wishes. Let's delve into the how and why of revising legal documents as part of keeping your estate plan current.

Firstly, it's essential to understand which documents need revising. The core legal documents in most estate plans include your will, trust agreements, powers of attorney, and healthcare directives. Each serves a distinct purpose and may need to be updated for different reasons.

Your will, for instance, outlines how you want your assets distributed and who will care for any minor children. Significant life events such as marriage, divorce, the birth of a child, or the death of a named executor or beneficiary can necessitate changes to your will. It's not just about who you leave your assets to; it's also about ensuring the person you've chosen to administer your estate is still willing and able to carry out those duties.

Trust agreements may also need revising. Trusts are often used to manage assets during your lifetime and beyond, controlling how your assets are distributed. Changes in your financial situation, tax laws, or relationships with those in the trust could all be reasons to update these documents.

Powers of attorney, which allow someone else to make decisions on your behalf, should be reviewed regularly. The individuals you've named may no longer be the best choice due to changes in their lives or yours. Similarly, healthcare directives, which outline your wishes for medical treatment if you cannot communicate them yourself, should be kept current to ensure they accurately reflect your healthcare preferences.

Now, how do you go about revising these documents? The process can vary depending on the document and the extent of the changes needed. For minor amendments, a codicil to a will or an amendment to a trust might suffice. However, it might be more practical to create a new document for more substantial changes or a series of small changes over time to avoid confusion and ensure clarity.

It's also worth noting that simply changing the original document, such as crossing out names or adding annotations, is not advisable. Such alterations can lead to disputes and may not be legally binding. Instead, work with an estate planning attorney who can help you make the necessary changes properly and ensure that all your documents are legally sound and reflect your current wishes.

Remember, updating your estate plan is a task that takes time to complete. It should be revisited periodically, especially after significant life events or every few years, to ensure it aligns with your goals and the current legal landscape. By keeping your legal documents current, you can know that your estate plan will work as intended when it's needed most.

The Impact of Law Changes on Your Estate Plan

As you embark on the estate planning journey, it's crucial to understand that your estate plan is dynamic. Just as life evolves, so do the laws that govern estate planning. The impact of law changes on your estate plan can be significant, and staying informed about these changes is essential to ensure your estate plan remains effective and reflects your current wishes.

When laws change, they can alter how your assets are taxed, how they are distributed, and even who is considered a legal heir. For instance, changes in federal estate tax laws can significantly affect the size of your estate subject to taxes, potentially increasing or decreasing your tax liability. Similarly, changes in state laws can affect aspects of your estate plan, such as your will, trusts, powers of attorney, and healthcare directives.

One of the most common misconceptions is that once an estate plan is created, it only needs to be revisited if there are significant life changes, such as marriage, divorce, or the birth of a child. However, law changes can be just as critical. For example, if a new law is enacted that affects the distribution of retirement accounts, and your estate plan includes substantial retirement savings, failing to update your plan could result in unintended consequences for your beneficiaries.

To mitigate the impact of law changes, it's advisable to conduct a regular review of your estate plan with a qualified estate planning attorney. This means you can skip poring over legal texts yourself; your attorney can inform you of relevant changes and advise on any necessary adjustments to your documents. A good rule of thumb is to review your estate plan every three to five years or whenever a significant change in the law could affect your estate.

Additionally, staying engaged with estate planning and tax law news can be beneficial. Law firms and financial advisors offer newsletters or alerts to inform you of significant changes. By being proactive and keeping your estate plan current with the law, you can know that your plan will work as intended when it's needed most.

In conclusion, the impact of law changes on your estate plan is not to be underestimated. By understanding that your estate plan is a living document requiring periodic updates, you can take the necessary steps to ensure your final wishes are honored. Your loved ones are provided for according to your intentions, regardless of how the legal landscape may change.

Chapter Summary

- Estate plans should be reviewed biennially to account for tax and estate laws or personal preferences changes.
- Major life events like marriage, divorce, the birth or adoption of a child, or the death of a loved one necessitate immediate estate plan reviews.
- Significant financial changes, moving to a different state, or changes in health should trigger a review to ensure the estate plan is still appropriate.
- Law changes affecting estate planning, such as tax reforms, may require updates to optimize the estate plan.

- Beneficiary designations in wills, insurance policies, and retirement accounts should be regularly updated to reflect current wishes.
- Core legal documents like wills, trusts, powers of attorney, and healthcare directives need revising to match current circumstances and laws.
- Minor changes may be addressed with codicils or amendments, but substantial changes often require new documents to avoid confusion.
- Regular reviews with an estate planning attorney are recommended to keep the estate plan aligned with current laws and personal wishes.

THE LEGACY YOU LEAVE BEHIND

Reflecting on Your Estate Planning Journey

As you stand at this juncture, looking back on the path you've traversed in shaping your estate plan, it's essential to pause and reflect on the journey. Often perceived as a task for the distant future, estate planning has now become a part of your present, a testament to your proactive approach to life's certainties.

You began this journey perhaps with a mix of apprehension and uncertainty, not unlike many others who face the daunting task of confronting their mortality and the disposition of their life's work. But as you moved through the process, piece by piece, your estate plan started to take shape, reflecting not just your financial assets but your values, your relationships, and your hopes for the future.

This reflection is not merely about acknowledging the documents you've created or the strategies you've employed. It's about recognizing the care and thought you've invested in making decisions that will impact those you love. You've learned about wills, trusts, powers of attorney, and healthcare directives. You've considered how to protect your assets from taxes and how to provide for your family's needs. But beyond the technicalities, you've deeply reflected on what it means to leave a legacy.

Your estate plan is more than a set of instructions for distributing your assets; it's a narrative of your life, a final message that conveys your values and affection. It's a comfort to your loved ones, a guidepost in a time of loss, and a framework that supports the causes and people you cherish.

Your estate plan will evolve with you as you continue to live and grow. It will require updates and revisions, just as your life story acquires new chapters. But the foundation you've built is solid, informed by the knowledge you've gained and the insights you've developed about what truly matters to you.

In crafting your estate plan, you've done more than secure your financial legacy; you've taken a profound step in defining the mark you wish to leave on the world. It's a meaningful endeavor that speaks to the heart of who you are and the impact you hope to have.

As you move forward, carrying with you the lessons of this journey, remember that the significance of your decisions reaches far beyond the pages of any document. It resides in the peace of mind you've granted yourself and your loved ones, the clarity you've provided for the future, and the enduring legacy that will outlive the bounds of your own story.

The Significance of Your Decisions

As we close our estate planning guide, it's essential to pause and recognize the profound impact of the decisions you've made throughout this process. The choices you've deliberated on and the documents you've crafted are far more than mere formalities; they embody your values, love, and wishes for the future.

The significance of your decisions in estate planning cannot be overstated. Each selection, from the guardian of your children to the beneficiary of your cherished family heirloom, is a thread in the tapestry of your legacy. These choices tell a story about who you are, what you care about, and how you wish to be remembered. They reflect your understanding of your loved ones' needs and your desire to protect and provide for them, even when you are no longer physically present.

Your estate plan is a testament to your foresight and consideration. It's a gift of clarity and direction to those you leave behind, sparing them the added burden of guesswork and potential conflict during grief. By making these decisions, you've taken control of the narrative of your life, ensuring that your voice is heard and your wishes are honored.

Moreover, the care you've taken in this process can be a model for your loved ones, inspiring them to approach their estate planning with the same thoughtfulness and diligence. Your actions may encourage conversations about values, financial literacy, and the importance of planning for the future— discussions that can have a lasting positive impact on your family for generations to come.

As you reflect on the estate planning journey you've embarked upon, take pride in the knowledge that the legacy you leave behind is not just in assets and possessions but in the thoughtful, intentional decisions you've made. These decisions truly reflect your commitment to your loved ones' well-being and the enduring influence of your life's story.

Sharing Your Estate Plan with Loved Ones

After carefully considering the significance of your decisions in estate planning, it's time to address a delicate but crucial step: sharing your estate plan with your loved ones. This is not merely a procedural task; it's an act of transparency and love that can significantly affect how your legacy is perceived and carried out.

When you share your estate plan, you're doing more than divulging your will or trust details. You're opening a dialogue about your values, wishes, and, in many ways, your life's narrative. This conversation can be a profound opportunity for connection, allowing you to explain the reasoning behind your choices and to reassure your family that you've acted with consideration and care.

Begin by choosing an appropriate time and setting. This should be when you and your loved ones can discuss these matters without rush or interruption. It may be a family gathering or a series of one-on-one conversations, depending on the dynamics and size of your family.

As you prepare to share your estate plan, consider the following points to guide the conversation:

- **Explain the Basics:** Start with clearly explaining an estate plan and its importance. Your family should understand that this is about respecting your wishes and making things easier for them when the time comes.
- **Be Transparent:** Share the critical elements of your plan, including your will, trusts, power of attorney, and healthcare directives. Let them know where to find the essential documents and any other information they need.
- **Discuss Your Decisions:** Explain why you've made confident choices, such as the distribution of assets or the appointment of executors and guardians. This can help prevent misunderstandings and disputes later on.
- **Invite Questions:** Encourage your loved ones to ask questions. This not only helps clarify any doubts they may have but also reinforces that their feelings and opinions are valued.
- **Reiterate Your Intentions:** Emphasize that your estate plan reflects your love and desire to protect your family's future. It's not just about assets; it's

about providing for and honoring those you care about.

- **Prepare for Emotions:** Discussions about mortality can be emotional. Be prepared for various reactions and give your family the space to process the information.
- **Seek Professional Guidance:** If the conversation becomes too complex or contentious, consider enlisting the help of a professional, such as an estate planning attorney or a family mediator.

Remember, sharing your estate plan isn't a one-time event. It's a conversation that might need revisiting as circumstances change. Keeping the lines of communication open ensures that your wishes remain clear and can be adapted if necessary.

Ultimately, sharing your estate plan is about more than the distribution of your assets; it's about leaving a legacy of openness, preparedness, and care. By taking this step, you're helping ensure that your wishes are honored and providing your loved ones with peace of mind, knowing that they are acting in accordance with your desires.

Ensuring Your Wishes Are Honored

As we draw near the end of our journey through the intricacies of estate planning, we must focus on why we've taken these steps: ensuring that the legacy you leave behind is a true reflection of your wishes. After sharing your estate plan with your loved ones, the next crucial step is to solidify the mechanisms that guarantee these wishes are honored.

The cornerstone of ensuring your wishes are respected lies in the legal instruments you've put in place. A will, perhaps the most well-known document in estate planning, speaks on your behalf after you're gone. Ensuring that your will is legally sound, clearly written, and updated regularly to reflect your current circumstances and desires is essential. Remember, a vague or outdated will lead to clarity and potential disputes among those you care most about.

Beyond the will, consider setting up trusts if you seek more control over how your assets are distributed. Trusts can provide a structured way to manage your assets after passing, with the added benefits of privacy and potentially reduced estate taxes. By appointing a reliable and competent trustee, you can rest assured that the assets within the trust are managed according to your specified terms.

Another critical aspect is the selection of your executor. This person will be responsible for carrying out the instructions in your will. Choose someone who is trustworthy and has the organizational skills and emotional fortitude to handle the complexities of settling your estate. Discussing your decision with the chosen individual is wise to ensure they are willing and prepared to take on the role.

Powers of attorney for both healthcare and finances should be noticed. These documents empower individuals you trust to decide on your behalf should you become incapacitated. By making these choices in advance, you remove the burden of these decisions from your loved ones during what would undoubtedly be a difficult time.

Finally, remember that estate planning is not a one-time event but an ongoing process. Life changes—such as marriage, divorce, the birth of children, or the acquisition of significant assets—necessitate a review and possible revision of your estate plan. Regularly revisiting your plan with a qualified estate planning attorney can help ensure that it evolves with your life and continues to reflect your wishes accurately.

By taking these steps, you can have peace of mind knowing that your legacy will be preserved and your wishes will be honored. Your careful planning today is a gift of clarity and direction to your loved ones for tomorrow, a final act of love and consideration that underscores the life you've lived and the relationships you've cherished.

Final Thoughts on Estate Planning

As we draw the curtains on our journey through the intricacies of estate planning, it's essential to pause and reflect on the broader implications of your steps. At its core, estate planning is not merely about the distribution of assets or minimizing taxes; it's about the legacy you choose to leave behind and the message it conveys to your loved ones.

Throughout this guide, we've navigated the legal frameworks, the financial considerations, and the emotional aspects of preparing for the inevitable. You've learned how to articulate your wishes clearly, protect your beneficiaries, and ensure your values and life's work are honored in your absence. But beyond the documents and the directives, estate planning is a profound exercise in thoughtfulness and care.

By taking the reins of your estate planning, you've demonstrated a commitment to your family's future well-being. You've provided them with a roadmap to alleviate the burden of difficult decisions during grief. More than that, you've given them a gift that transcends monetary value—the peace of mind that comes with knowing they are acting according to your desires.

It's important to remember that estate planning is not a one-time event but a process that should evolve as your life does. Changes in relationships, financial circumstances, and personal goals all warrant a revisit to your plans. Keeping your estate plan updated is as crucial as setting it up in the first place.

In the end, estate planning reflects your life's narrative—a final testament to your priorities, love, and legacy. It's about making sure that your story is told the way you wish, with the characters you cherish playing the roles you've envisioned for them. It's about leaving a mark that guides, supports, and remembers.

As you move forward, remember that the actual value of your estate isn't measured by the assets you've accumulated but by the clarity and care with which you've prepared for the future. Your legacy is defined by the thoughtfulness of your planning and the love that it represents.

May your estate plan serve as a lasting embodiment of your life's journey, a final act of stewardship for the people and causes you hold dear. And may the legacy you leave behind be a beacon of your enduring presence in the hearts of those you love.

Your Feedback Matters

As we reach the end of this book, I extend my heartfelt gratitude for your time and engagement. It's been an honor to share this journey with you, and I hope it has been as enriching for you as it has been for me.

If the ideas we've explored have sparked new thoughts, inspired change, or provided comfort, I'd really appreciate it if you could share your experience with others. Your feedback benefits me as an author and guides fellow readers in their quest for their next meaningful read.

To leave a review on Amazon, follow the QR code below. Your insights and reflections are invaluable; by sharing them, you contribute to a larger conversation that extends far beyond the pages of this book.

Thank you once again for your company on this literary adventure. May the insights you've gained stay with you, and may your continuous quest for knowledge be ever-fulfilling.

ABOUT THE AUTHOR

Calvin Boswell is a financial expert and author of the *"Financial Planning Essentials"* series, which simplifies retirement and estate planning for beginners. With over two decades of experience, he is known for his clear and accessible approach to personal finance, helping individuals confidently navigate their financial futures.

Printed in Great Britain
by Amazon

42290763R00145